# TO SURVIVE CAREGIVING

*A Daughter's Experience,*
*A Doctor's Advice*

Second Edition

CHERYL E. WOODSON, MD, FACP, AGSF, CHCQM
*Family Caregiver, Geriatrician*

Dr. Cheryl Woodson

Category: Non-Fiction/Self-Help-Caregiving/Geriatrics
ISBN: 978-0-996-7809-0-2    paperback
ISBN: 978-0-9967809-3-3    e-book

Second Edition-Revised and Updated November 2021

# TABLE OF CONTENTS

# Give Power To Your Caregiving

I developed two special concepts to give you more power in caregiving: the *Five Keys to Caregiver Survival and the Level of Care Prescription (LOCRx)*. If you take nothing else from this book, please hold on to the Five Keys. I developed them to show you how to give excellent eldercare without killing yourself. Although I explain the Five Keys thoroughly in Chapter 8, I list them here for your convenience.

**The Five Keys to Caregiver Survival**

1. **Don't Stick Your Head in the Sand.** According to folklore, ostriches do this because they think the danger can't see them if they can't see the danger. Not! *Find out if you need help.*

2. **Take the "S" off Your Chest or Step Away from the Kryptonite.** You are not *Supercaregiver! You DO Need Help.*

3. **"Don't Ask, Don't Tell" Won't Work.** This key includes several points to help you decide how to tell, whom to tell, and how to deal with the responses. *Tell people you need help.*

4. **If You Don't Want to Drive All the Time, Take Your Hands Off the Steering Wheel.** Do you discourage people who would help? *Let people help.*

5. **Put Your Mask on First.** This is what airline flight attendants tell you to do in an emergency. *You can't take care of THEM if you don't take care of YOU.*

### Level of are Prescription (LOCRx)

This tool can soothe the worry, fear, and guilt caregivers feel when they wonder whether they are giving the right care. Though your health care team does not use the term, "LOCRx" (I created it for you), they will be able to answer the specific questions I'll teach you to ask in Chapter 4: *Don't Despair - There IS Help*. The answers will show you exactly what your loved one needs. This information will also boost your confidence and reassure you that you are giving the best possible care.

### Another new resource: *The Doctor is IN*

Since I published the first edition of *To Survive Caregiving* in 2006, caregivers in my medical practice and attendees at my national presentations have raised excellent questions. For example: "How do we decide whether Mom should live with us?" "What do we do when Dad overspends and asks us to pay his living expenses every month while we have kids, a mortgage, and other bills?" One of the most poignant questions concerns the painful challenge of people whose spouses have dementia. I believe each of these caregivers is "Another Kind of Widow."

Caregivers have told me other authors don't seem to discuss these topics, yet the questions deserve serious thought and well-developed answers. Since these specific topics are beyond the scope of *To Survive Caregiving*, I wrote a new companion book, *The Doctor is IN: Answering Your Questions About How to Survive Caregiving*. Here, you will find extensive discussions about these and other specific caregiver concerns. Your copy is available at Amazon.com and other booksellers right now.

### You *are* a caregiver.

No matter the person's age, their level of ability, or your relationship with them, if you take care of *anything* for people who cannot meet *all* their own needs, *you are a caregiver*. Whether you live across the room, across town, or across the country, whether you give hands-on care or organize and supervise, you are a caregiver, and this book is for you.

Many people are frightened by reports that the needs of older Americans are skyrocketing along with their numbers. The media and some specialists in aging have called this phenomenon the "Silver Tsunami." In the wake of this huge wave, our families, communities, healthcare system, and other businesses are in danger of drowning. You are one of the millions of family caregivers who provide more than seventy percent of all eldercare in this country. Though you struggle to surf the "Silver Tsunami," don't be afraid. In this book, I offer you a surfboard.

My goals are to:

- Erase your guilt.

- Encourage you.

- Give you permission to take care of yourself.

- Provide the information you need to give excellent care without sacrificing your physical, financial, emotional, or spiritual health.

- Arm you with tools that empower you to become an effective activist for causes that affect both seniors and other caregivers.

**I'm here for you.**

I spent more than thirty years teaching and practicing Geriatric Medicine (the care of older adults). During those years, I saw families crushed by caregiving responsibility. I experienced my own caregiving challenges as I navigated my mother's ten-year journey with Alzheimer's disease. Just like many of you, other responsibilities competed for my energy. I had a spouse, kids, a job, and I was active in my church and community. I also had stress, pain, fear, confusion, and guilt.

In addition to my professional and personal eldercare experience, I have had the privilege of working with some amazing caregivers in a variety of practice settings. I am honored to have walked with these families though difficult situations. I am also grateful that we walked together into the victory of giving excellent eldercare without destroying the caregivers' health, finances, or relationships.

Professional training gave me medical knowledge and inside information about how to get things done in our confusing health care system. Personal caregiving experience and sharing the journeys of other successful caregivers gave me practical applications. I wrote this book to share all of this with you.

Let my experience as daughter and doctor validate your feelings, confirm your decisions, and comfort you as you travel along your caregiving path. I offer a shoulder to lean on, a lap to sit in, a voice in your ear, and a guiding hand at your back as you deal with the difficult decisions. I also hope to give you a chuckle to lighten your load along the way.

**This is *not* your mama's caregiving.**

Most caregivers feel so guilty. As they remember that their parents cared for their grandparents, they worry that they cannot give care as well as their parents did. These new caregivers don't understand that *it* isn't the same thing at all. No previous generation has faced the challenges that confront today's caregivers.

**You have your hands full!**

You care for parents, in-laws, and other seniors while raising children and grandchildren. All this happens while you work, try to stay married, have a life, and plan for your own senior years. You struggle to get doctors to talk to you in English, not Doctorspeak, and you're in the dark about the help available in your communities. You also toil under the weight of guilt trips other people lay on you. These mouthy folks don't like what you're doing but most of the time, they won't step up to help you. Whew! No wonder you're tired. This is not fair; it's not necessary, and you don't have to put up with it.

**You're taking care of *them* and killing *yourself*.**

You're doing everything. You get your seniors to their doctors' appointments on time and make sure they have all the recommended tests and procedures. You pick up their prescriptions and see that they take every medicine in the right amount, at the right time, and according to the doctor's instructions. You guarantee that your seniors eat the right foods, in the right portions, and you find ways to give them exercise, company, and entertainment. You keep their homes in order and in good repair. You are careful to use their money wisely and pay their bills on time, but aren't you forgetting something?

How well do you take care of your loved ones' most important asset: the one that makes everything else possible? *How well do you take care of their caregiver?* What about *your* doctor appointments, preventive health screening, other tests, and prescriptions? What about *your* nutrition, fitness, finances, and family? You're so busy giving care that you don't usually take time to step back and look at what *you* need.

**Supporting them should not equal suicide.**

Caregiving should not make you sick. Nor should it mean the death of your career, your marriage, or other relationships. You should not have to sacrifice your finances or your joy. I want to help you find ways to put yourself higher up on the To-Do list. You can have a full life while giving the best possible care.

**These are *real* caregiver stories.**

I illustrate each topic with information shared by the caregivers I've known over the years or from my own caregiving experiences. (Asterisks separate the stories from the discussions.) I have changed names and other identifying details to respect these caregivers' privacy. None of the names refer to persons of the same names, either living or dead, therefore, any similarity is coincidental and totally unintentional. In some cases, to illustrate a specific point, I have condensed and combined the experiences of several families. Even so, the challenges and solutions are *real*. I believe you will see yourself in at least some of these stories.

**This book isn't about illness. It's about caregiving.**

Instead of focusing on specific diseases, my goal is to empower you to handle any condition that challenges you and your loved ones. However, many caregivers support older relatives with Alzheimer's disease and other dementias. They ask questions about these devastating illnesses at my seminars. Because of this and because my own caregiving involved a parent with Alzheimer's disease, several of the stories in *To Survive Caregiving* involve families living with memory loss. With this one exception, the book does not highlight a specific illness. The discussions will help regardless of the conditions your loved ones face. The age of the people you support does not matter either. The information will help you care for seniors, younger adults, and even children who live with chronic health challenges.

**Caregiving is more than a set of tasks.**

I don't offer long checklists. I won't tell you how to dress wounds or give treatments. I am not going to teach you about specific medicines. Though I mention Medicare, other health insurance plans, and the Affordable Care Act, I don't go into deep discussions about these topics. If I did, those sections would take over the book! *To Survive Caregiving* offers information to strengthen your caregiving skills and:

- Explain why caregiving is more challenging today than it was in past generations
- Teach you how to get doctors to *really* listen, explain care plans, and offer frank discussions of changes that may come down the road
- Describe how doctors and other eldercare professionals can stand with you or in front of you when your family gives you a hard time
- Show you how to find eldercare resources in your community
- Offer specific strategies that increase your chances of getting help from other family members

You say there aren't any other family members? I have practical solutions for you whether you're the only child or the only child who's doing anything. This book will also suggest better ways to communicate with seniors and encourage their cooperation, but ultimately this book isn't about the people you care for.


**This one's for *you*.**

I intend to build your confidence, convince you that you can give excellent care, and show you how to protect *your* health, finances, and relationships along the way. By addressing how you feel about your responsibilities, I will assure you that *anything* you feel is okay. However, I will challenge you to work through potentially destructive feelings so you can:

- Release anger (It hurts only *you*).
- Stop majoring in the minor (worrying about things that don't really matter).
- Stop wasting time and energy being angry with other family members or trying to make them feel guilty.
- Tap into your support team.
- Recognize when your problems are self-made.
- Teach you how to get out of your own way.
- CREATE JOY!

**Use this book the way you need to.**

Read straight through or explore specific topics as they come up in the course of your caregiving. Read the family stories and decide whether you identify with the struggles they describe, or skip ahead to the discussions.

If you're not interested in public policy, you may want to skip the first and last sections. I hope you won't. Current eldercare policy is outdated and fails seniors and their caregivers. This will not change until policies reflect the way Americans age *today*, support everyone who lives with chronic illness, and respect the challenges that confront current caregivers. *You* are the most credible and powerful force in encouraging legislators to make policies that really work. The chapters in Sections I and V will give you the ammunition you need to be a more effective advocate.

**I heard you.**

Although this second edition of *To Survive Caregiving* is updated, revised, and expanded, thanks to feedback from caregivers, I have included fewer statistics. Every year, AARP and the National Alliance for Caregiving publish *Caregiving in the Unites States*. This thorough report gives updated details on the number of caregivers, who and where they are, their responsibilities, health, and financial resources. It is available every spring and can provide any data you need.

I will continue to focus on showing you that your fears, fatigue, confusion, and even your anger *make sense*. I want to assure you that *nothing* can prevent you from giving the best possible care, and I intend to *empower* you to do so while you also take care of yourself.

I have made it easier to find the resources you need by grouping similar topics into the five sections that:

- Describe the caregiving challenge.

- Offer strategies that empower you to be a more effective caregiver.

- Define the impact of caregiving on caregivers and teach you how to protect yourself.

- Arm you to wrestle with some of the most painful decisions in caregiving.

- Prepare you to become an activist in developing public policies that benefit everyone as we age.

I still discuss strategies to protect your physical, financial, emotional, and spiritual health. However, instead of repeating a comprehensive review of health and wellness in this edition, the "Physical Health" chapter explains what happens to caregivers who don't take care of themselves. It also recommends how to care for your senior's caregiver. That's YOU!

For a thorough discussion of specific health and wellness strategies that apply to you, I refer you to your primary care professional. Please visit my website, www.drcherylwoodson.com, to request my free information sheet, "*You Should Know These Numbers Like You Know Your Social Security Number.*" This form lists all the current health screening guidelines. Discuss this form with your health care team, and review it at least every year. I invite you to also follow my blog, *Straight Talk with Dr. Cheryl,* to learn how to *LIVE OUT LOUD AND AGE EXCELLENTLY.*

## A bit of housekeeping

Many caregivers told me that much of the information in my books and presentations is new to them. Many of us learn best by repetition, and there is value in emphasizing topics through different perspectives. For this reason, I present similar information in several parts of the book using different stories and discussions.

As in the first edition, instead of using the cumbersome "he or she," "him or her," and "his or hers," unless a sentence refers to a specific person, or the information applies to men and women differently, I will alternate pronouns throughout the text.

## More housekeeping

The Leaders of Aging Organizations, the Reframing Aging Project, and the Frameworks Institute produced the report, *Gauging Aging: Mapping the Gaps Between Expert and Public Understandings of Aging in America* (www.frameworksinstitute.org/publication/gauging-aging-mapping-the-gaps-between-expert-and-public-understandings-of-aging-in-america).

This publication demonstrates the need to emphasize the diversity and contributions of older people. It recommends that professionals who advocate for the aged show how policies that benefit older Americans can make life better for everyone. The report also shows that the language professionals in aging use to describe the needs of older adults can undermine our advocacy. It says terms like "exploding needs" may discourage younger adults and decrease their support for older people.

No matter what you call it, I believe our nation *is* ill-prepared for the growing number of older adults. Unless we face this truth and begin to prepare, their needs *will* overwhelm the resources of our health system, housing industry, the workplace and overall economy, our families, and communities.

Although I agree words like "Silver Tsunami," may turn off folks who fear getting wet, *To Survive Caregiving* speaks to people who are already struggling to tread water. I use terms that show caregivers I understand their challenge. Caregivers can *surf* the Silver Tsunami and as I said, I offer this book as a surfboard.

Based on *Gauging Aging*, some advocates also disparage terms like "senior," "elder," and "older adult." I disagree with them because to me and many others, "senior" and "elder" are not negatives. A senior advisor is not decrepit; she is experienced. An elder is someone who has earned respect and has wisdom to impart. My 94-year-old Aunt Terri worked until the pandemic and walks seventeen laps around her building every day. My mentor, Mrs. Wilma Jenkins, insists that omitting 84 years *old* negates her wisdom. I want to be *them* when I grow up! They show that being an older adult is a blessing so, I will continue to use the words I have always used.

The resource list contains materials I found helpful in my own caregiving and those I shared with the caregivers in my medical practice. Many other excellent and more current resources are available to you. I encourage you to explore and share the ones you find helpful.

**You *can* do this.**

Caregiving can be stressful, especially when you try to juggle many responsibilities. Once you learn what to do and how to get the help you need, you can leave worry and guilt behind. Then, you can move into successful caregiving and healthy *living*. That means handling your responsibilities more easily and finding time to create joy for yourself.

Though many of us feel honored and happy to give care, sometimes even under the best circumstances, we can feel angry, overwhelmed, resentful, or scared. *It's okay.* What you *feel* does not have to dictate what you *do*. You can give exceptional care despite complex, conflicting, or painful feelings, and you can do it without destroying yourself.

You can survive caregiving and find hope, help, and health. Come and share my practical experiences as a daughter while also getting professional advice from me as a doctor.

You can do this! Let me help you.

# SECTION I

# The Crisis in Caregiving

So many caregivers have told me, "My mother took care of my grandmother! Why am I so tired?" It's no wonder that you're tired because:

- This is *not* your mama's caregiving.
- You have more on your plate.
- You have a smaller plate.

# CHAPTER 1

# The Growing Needs of America's Seniors: "The Silver Tsunami"

Many caregivers feel guilty when they admit to being overwhelmed. They feel especially bad when older relatives say, "I don't see what you're complaining about. We always took care of everybody ourselves. Our family doesn't put people in nursing homes or hire strangers."

They say hindsight is 20/20. It also sees through rose-colored lenses. The truth is, families did not always do what they say they did. Even if their memories are correct, the caregiving responsibility of past generations was not as intense as the challenges that face today's caregivers. Twenty-first century caregivers are responsible for *MORE* older adults, *OLDER* older adults, and *SICKER* older adults than past generations of caregivers. The responsibility has grown despite shrinking caregiving resources. In other words, today there is a Crisis in Caregiving.

### *The Wave – MORE Older Adults*

The needs of American seniors are increasing with their numbers. Journalists and professionals in aging have coined the term "Silver Tsunami" to describe the impact of this growing number of older adults. This wave threatens to drown families, communities, the healthcare system, and other businesses.

The number of Americans over age sixty-five increased from about thirty-seven million in 2006 to forty-nine million in 2016. That represents an increase of about thirty-three percent, while the population under age sixty-five increased only about five percent.$_{(1)}$ Future statistics will be even more dramatic because of the impact of the Baby Boomers, people born between 1946 and 1964. At each stage of their lives, the Baby Boomers were the largest group in American history: the largest group of babies, children, teenagers, college students, and so on. When the first Baby Boomers reached age sixty-five in 2011, they became the largest group of senior citizens our nation has ever seen. About ten thousand Americans reach age sixty-five every day and statisticians expect this to continue through 2030.$_{(2)}$ The increasing number of seniors is only part of the challenge.

### The Older You Get, The Older You Get:
### *OLDER Older Adults*

A white woman born in 1946 was expected to live about seventy years.$_{(3)}$ Today, that woman is seventy-five-years-old. The statistics say that when she was sixty-five, she could have expected to live to age eighty-five (another twenty years).$_{(4)}$ If she lives to eighty-five, she has a greater chance of living to 100 than was expected when she was sixty-five. The percentage of Americans over age 100 increased almost forty-five percent between 2000 and 2014.$_{(5)}$

At each stage of life, people have a greater chance of living long enough to reach the next age milestone because they outlive illnesses that would have killed them. (These include heart disease, cancer, lung disease, accidents, stroke, Alzheimer's disease, diabetes, infections, kidney disease, suicide, violence, and other conditions).$_{(6)}$ Even though we are living longer, it is not clear that Americans are living better.

### Have We Gained Time, or Are We Doing Time?
### *SICKER Older Adults*

In the first half of the twentieth century, the major causes of death were infections.[7] Back then, when people got sick, they either got better or they died. Today, many do neither.

Instead of dying quickly from sudden episodes of severe illness, people live for years with increasing disability from chronic conditions. This is because of public health initiatives and medical advances that occurred over the past eighty years or so. Some of the innovations that have staved off death include:

- Better nutrition and sanitation
- Antibiotics
- Blood transfusion
- Cancer chemotherapy and other powerful medicines
- Artificial respiration (ventilators), feeding tubes, and dialysis (to treat kidney failure)
- Cardiopulmonary resuscitation (CPR)
- Organ transplants
- Procedures that open blocked blood vessels
- Heart pumps and defibrillators (mechanical devices that support failing hearts and correct dangerous heartbeats)

Medical miracles involve tests and treatments that require machines and advanced medicines. Though these strategies can prolong life, they do not always improve health. This can make people wish they were dead because they live long enough to experience a slow, painful decline from incurable illnesses that would have brought a quick death in the past. For example, instead of dying from a sudden heart attack, people survive with sick hearts that pump much less blood than a healthy heart. Despite medicine, these hearts provide so little energy that some people find it difficult to eat and breathe at the same time.

Chronic diseases cause suffering and rob people of their independence and their joy. They do the same to caregivers when they compare themselves with past generations of caregivers. This is unfair because the former caregivers did not have to deal with the same amount of chronic disease. While additional medical advancements and wellness initiatives may change the level of disability in future seniors, today's caregivers have more responsibility. They serve *more* older adults who are *older, sicker,* and have *higher* care needs for a *longer* time. This responsibility also falls on fewer shoulders than in the past, Those shoulders are also narrower because of competing responsibilities that previous generations did not have.

# CHAPTER 2

# You Are Doing More With Less:
## *Shrinking Caregiver Resources*

I intend neither sexism nor disrespect to the husbands, sons, and other male relatives who give excellent care and constitute about forty percent of caregivers. I have had little experience with transgender, intersex, or non-binary caregivers. In this discussion, I focus on women not only because that was the caregiving experience in my family but also because historically and still by majority, the term "caregiver" has equaled unpaid, female relative.

About sixty percent of seniors who receive care and sixty-two percent of caregivers, are female.[8] Women are in the workforce in greater numbers than ever before, yet as Arlie Hochschild and Ann Machungh said in their book, *The Second Shift: Working Families and the Revolution at Home*, working women also bear the brunt of responsibility for housekeeping, childcare and now, eldercare.[9]

## Five Generations of Caregiving in an American Family—Mine

 Fannie Morgan was my great-grandmother, and everybody called her "Grandmom." She had eleven children; six were alive when she needed care and four were daughters. At that time, none of Grandmom's daughters worked outside the home, and no one lived more than five miles away. Grandmom lived with one of her daughters in a household that also included three adult grandchildren (the youngest of whom was almost thirty years old) and two great-grandchildren, ages eight and ten.

Grandmom's illness lasted about a month before she died of "old age" (probably pneumonia related to a stroke).

 Eula Cothran (called "Mom"), my grandmother, was Grandmom's primary caregiver. When Mom needed care for herself, she also had six children including four daughters. Mom's primary caregiver was a daughter who lived in the same house. An adult son and two grandchildren, age nineteen and twenty-one also lived in the home. Two more daughters, another son, and a daughter-in-law lived within walking distance; the fourth daughter lived about five miles away. During Mom's illness, her youngest grandchild was eleven years old.

Mom's primary caregiver worked part-time. Another daughter was a full-time homemaker who lived around the corner. The other two daughters worked full-time though neither put in more than forty hours per week. Mom's illness lasted about four months before she died of pancreatic cancer. However, on the day she died, Mom had felt well enough to cook Easter dinner for the extended family.

 My mother, Beatrice Woodson ("Mother") was the third of Mom's daughters, and she died after a ten-year struggle with Alzheimer's disease. In the caregiver situation, she was not as lucky as Grandmom and Mom had been. Mother had two children and only one was a daughter. For much of Mother's illness, I lived almost 800 miles away. My brother, Drexel, lived over 2000 miles away; for a time, he was out of the country.

I worked more than sixty hours per week, first on the faculty of two university medical schools, then in solo, private practice. My children were two and five years old when Mother first came to live with us. They were nine and twelve when she died. During this time, I also helped with the hands-on care of my mother-in-law and gave information and support to my cousins who watched over the aunts and uncles back home in Philadelphia, PA.

I may not be any luckier than Mother was. I also have only two children and was thirty-nine-years-old when I had my daughter. Because I waited so long to start my family, if I get sick at age sixty-nine (when Mother did,) my daughter may not have finished her education, or she could be in the developmental stages of her career. If she has children by then, they could be even younger than she and her brother were during my mother's illness.

\*\*\*\*\*\*\*\*\*\*\*\*\*\*\*\*\*\*\*\*\*\*\*\*\*\*

Current reports show that the number of caregivers in this country is increasing along with the level and length of their responsibility and the negative impact on their health and finances. In the past, the average caregiver was a fifty-six-year-old married (or otherwise partnered) working woman. Current reports show that the number of caregivers is increasing for all adult generations. Millennials (Americans born between 1980 and 2000) and even younger adults are giving care. Maybe they came back home (because of the pandemic, crushing educational debt, unemployment, or underemployment) and found that Mom or Grandpa needed more help than they knew.

About half of all caregivers support seniors who need help with at least two activities of daily living (moving in bed, dressing, bathing, getting to the bathroom, and other self-care tasks). About three quarters give care for at least five years while they work and put in about twenty more hours of caregiving per week. If a caregiver supports a person with Alzheimer's disease, she can easily exceed eighty weekly caregiving hours, and the years of caregiving can double to ten and beyond.[10, 11]

The term "Sandwich Generation" describes adults who are squeezed between responsibility for their parents and their children. The twenty-first-century Caregiver Sandwich is a multi-decker club! A caregiver in her fifties may support two seventy-year-olds, a ninety-year-old, people in their twenties, teenagers, young children, and babies all *at the same time.*

Parental death, deportation, substance abuse, incarceration, physical and mental illness, divorce, and financial hardship (debt, under- and unemployment) often leave children essentially orphaned. Grandparents stand in the gap. The number of adults with primary responsibility for grandchildren (or other relatives' children) doubled between 1970 and 2011. In about twenty percent of these households, neither of the children's parents were in the home.[12]

\*\*\*\*\*\*\*\*\*\*\*\*\*\*\*\*\*\*\*\*\*\*\*\*\*

Mrs. Marge Foley is a former patient and caregiver from my medical practice. She is the poster child for the twenty-first century Sandwich Generation challenge. Marge has anchored *five* generations. I met her in 1994 when she helped her mom care for her step-father through a cancer diagnosis. She also helped care for her grandmother who lived to be 104 years old. Over the years, in addition to her grandmother and parents, Marge participated in the care of a brother, an adult son, and several grandchildren. As Grandma to Millennials who have larger educational debt and poorer job opportunities than previous generations, Marge said she expected to help with great-grandchildren too.

\*\*\*\*\*\*\*\*\*\*\*\*\*\*\*\*\*\*\*\*\*\*\*\*\*

Today, there are more seniors than ever before. They live longer with serious illnesses that require increasing amounts of care over many years. Unfortunately, there are fewer potential caregivers to share the load. Most families have fewer children who as adults, live around the country, not around the corner. They also have responsibilities outside of caregiving including: childcare, employment, and planning for retirement. In some cases, they do all this while also fighting to avoid the emotional and financial upheaval of Gray Divorce, the increasing number of people who end their marriages later in life. [13] Those who have been able to win that battle still struggle to find time to invest in their relationships and take care of themselves.

*This has to change.*

In this first section, you learned about the Crisis in Caregiving, a situation that causes fear, anxiety, and guilt for caregivers who think they fall short in comparison to past caregivers. To be a confident caregiver, you need to learn what you *should* be doing, figure out whether it is possible for you to do it, and find the right people and resources to help you.

Section II will walk you through that process.

# You Can Meet the Challenge of Caregiving

Even though we've seen that you have more responsibility and less help, you're working hard to do your best. In this section, you'll learn:

- DON'T DENY - Recognize and accept that your senior needs help.

- DON'T DELAY - Move quickly to define the care need, set reasonable goals for what you can do, and make specific plans.

- DON'T DESPAIR – You are not alone. Learn how to get the help you need from professionals, your family, and your seniors.

# CHAPTER 3

# Don't Deny. Don't Delay:
## *See the Needs and Get Help NOW!*

When people begin to have physical, mental, or functional challenges, families can ignore the changes. This wastes valuable time.

**D'Nile Is Not Just a River... Stay Out of Egypt.**

Families in denial are unwilling or unable to accept that a problem exists.

*************************

Mrs. Miller lived alone for twenty years after her husband's death. She was active in her church and community and had a wide circle of friends. Her son, Robert, was a busy stockbroker who lived in another state. He called his mother weekly. Either she visited him, or he came to see her several times each year. Although Mrs. Miller had been a snappy dresser, she began to attend church wearing soiled clothes in clashing colors. She showed up a day early or a week late for church functions. She volunteered to label food baskets for the poor and could not follow the directions; her baskets always missed several items or had too many of the same things.

Mrs. Miller never seemed to have any money. Where she had always insisted on splitting costs fairly, she began to tell friends she had forgotten to go to the bank or had left her wallet at home. She could never pay her portion for trips, theatre tickets, and meals. Despite promising to repay her friends, she never did.

After one outing, Mrs. Miller pulled out of the church parking lot without looking and almost hit a car. She turned in the wrong direction and friends had to flag her down, turn her around, and show her how to get home. The friends worried that Mrs. Miller might get lost and started to pick her up for outings.

One evening, the friends came to take Mrs. Miller to a church concert and as the group prepared to leave, a young man rang the bell. Mrs. Miller immediately ran back into the house and brought him twenty dollars. When questioned, she laughed and said, "Today's his birthday. I always give the kids a buck or two."

Although Mrs. Miller's friends called Robert several times, he never took their concerns seriously. He always found a way to explain the changes in his mother's behavior.

"Your mom wanted to mail your little boy's birthday gift," a worried friend told Robert. "She was writing the label in pencil. I asked why she didn't use a magic marker, and she had no idea what a magic marker was!"

"Mom never has to mail packages," Robert answered, "Why should she know what a magic marker is?" When the friends informed him about the driving problems and the incidents at church, he dismissed those concerns too. "Mom didn't get lost. She was just upset by almost having an accident and got a little turned around. The church baskets aren't problems either. She was probably tired. It makes since that she would make little mistakes." Neither was he concerned about the young man who came to get money. "Mom's just being generous," he said.

Several weeks later, when Mrs. Miller's friends came to take her to another outing, the young man they had seen before answered the door. He would not let them in, but they could hear loud music and caught glimpses of several other young adults in the living room. When the friends returned with the police, they found Mrs. Miller alone and crying with bruises on her face and arms. Her refrigerator and freezer were empty; her television and jewelry were gone. Someone had emptied her purse onto the floor, and her cash and credit cards were missing.

Mrs. Miller went to stay with one of her friends. Her son came to town a few days later and found *stacks of unpaid bills, an empty bank account, and almost $30,000 in credit card debt.*

\*\*\*\*\*\*\*\*\*\*\*\*\*\*\*\*\*\*\*\*\*\*\*\*\*\*

Out-of-town family members are often unwilling or unable to accept that a senior is in trouble. When I was in practice, many families called to request a geriatrics consultation after holidays. Visiting family had called Mom every week and when they'd asked, "Howya doin' Mom?" she had always answered, "Fine, thank you, and you?" She also kept up other general pleasantries, and no one worried until they came home and found her wearing the same outfit every day. They were surprised to find burned pots on the stove, rotten food in the fridge, and stacks of bill collection notices.

Sometimes the home folks are unaware of problems even though they see the person every day. A senior may change so gradually that instead of taking notice, the local family starts giving support without being aware of it. For example, when nearby family notices that Mom wears the same outfit, they may start laying out her clothes.

Family members often disagree about whether a senior has a problem. These disagreements can bring out hidden family conflicts.

\*\*\*\*\*\*\*\*\*\*\*\*\*\*\*\*\*\*\*\*\*\*\*\*\*\*

Mr. Richards had four children. His son, Quentin, and his daughter, Daria, live out of town; two other daughters, Francine and Gwen, live near their dad. One Thanksgiving, Mr. Richards was late picking Quentin up at the airport and made several wrong turns on the way home. He declined his son's offer to drive and said, "I just got a little turned around, is all." Even so, Quentin had to direct his father to the correct route several times.

Quentin mentioned his concerns to Francine and suggested their dad see a doctor. She started yelling, "Just because you have all that money and live over there in that big house, don't think you can come in here and tell me what to do. I'm here every day, and I do everything for him."

Daria made the two-hour drive with her family. After dinner, she and her baby sister were cleaning the kitchen when Mr. Richards came in, carrying the leftover turkey. He started to put the platter in the cabinet under the sink, instead of in the refrigerator. The three of them laughed until he went into the living room to watch TV. Then, Gwen said, "See, that's what I've been telling you guys. He just isn't himself."

Daria slammed the cabinet door and turned to her sister. "Gwen, you just want Daddy to be sick so you can get his money. You never had to work for anything. He bought you a car and paid for your education. The rest of us rode the bus and we're *still* paying college loans. Isn't that enough for you?"

\*\*\*\*\*\*\*\*\*\*\*\*\*\*\*\*\*\*\*\*\*\*\*\*\*\*

Underlying family conflict can contribute to denial. In the Richards family, resentment about personal finances (Francine and Quentin) and perceived unequal and unfair treatment (Daria and Gwen) made it difficult for family members to even hear each other's concerns.

### Does Denial Protect You from Pain or Only Delay It?

Even without family issues, it is easy to understand why people are in denial. The moment you accept that there *is* a problem, your life, as you know it, is over. For the rest of your senior's life, eldercare will be on your To Do list-- right up there with the other responsibilities that already overwhelm you.

Some families deny because they want to avoid the emotional pain of accepting frailty in a respected elder. They may also want to avoid facing changes in the relationship.

\*\*\*\*\*\*\*\*\*\*\*\*\*\*\*\*\*\*\*\*\*\*\*\*\*\*

Seven years into a ten years of caregiving, my mother looked at me and said, "Do I know you?" When I heard those words come out of my mother's mouth, I thought I was going to die.

\*\*\*\*\*\*\*\*\*\*\*\*\*\*\*\*\*\*\*\*\*\*\*\*\*\*

Why wouldn't someone want to avoid that kind of pain? The problem is, the denial lasts only until an emergency forces you to address the changes. By that time, the situation can be much worse than it would have been had you acted earlier.

### Avoid Ageism: *"Age Is Not a Disease"* (The Late Maggie Kuhn, Founder of the Gray Panthers)

Denial is one barrier to acknowledging care needs. Ageism is another.

Ageism is a bias against older adults. It is also the expectation that elders *should* be disabled. Many families, professionals, and even seniors themselves believe "just getting old" explains any new problem. Ageism can lead families and professionals to underestimate the importance of changes in a senior's health and behavior. Lowered expectations create another barrier to acknowledging needs. This causes everyone to miss opportunities to protect a senior's health and independence.

\*\*\*\*\*\*\*\*\*\*\*\*\*\*\*\*\*\*\*\*\*\*\*\*\*

Mrs. Reese is a seventy-five-year-old woman who is active in her local drama and line-dancing group. Over several months, knee pain interfered with her dancing. Mrs. Reese, her family, and her doctor thought slowing down was to be expected at her age. After another few months sitting on the sidelines, Mrs. Reese stopped driving to performances and refused rides from friends. Her family assumed she was tired and needed "more rest at her age." Soon she withdrew from all social activities and spent more time alone sitting in front of the TV. When her family visited, they noticed that Mrs. Reese seemed surprised to see them, even though they always called to say they were coming. Her previously pristine housekeeping and personal care had also deteriorated. The family assumed she was "just getting senile."

Mrs. Reese called 9-1-1 because of sudden chest pain and shortness of breath. Inactivity had caused a blood clot to form in her leg, and the clot traveled to her lung. After a several days in the hospital on blood thinners, Mrs. Reese was too weak to go home alone. The family decided to move her into permanent long-term care.

The care team requested consultation from Physical Medicine and Rehabilitation (P M & R) specialists (physiatrists) who are skilled in testing all aspects of physical and mental function. The physiatrists made the diagnosis of depression. Mrs. Reese received psychotherapy, antidepressant medicine, and physical therapy. After strengthening her knee and regaining her stamina, she returned home with an exercise program and ongoing counseling. Mrs. Reese's memory, mobility, and spirit improved. Though she still needs to ice her knee sometimes, she is dancing again.

\*\*\*\*\*\*\*\*\*\*\*\*\*\*\*\*\*\*\*\*\*\*\*\*\*

Despite the media blitz for products that promise to make us more youthful, aging is *not* optional. Mature bodies *are* different. Older adults recover from illness more slowly and may have severe reactions to situations that wouldn't affect younger adults. Although the "seasoned saints" may not perform activities as *quickly* as younger people, when there is not an illness, other stressors, or time pressure, older adults can perform as *well* as younger ones. Healthy seniors are not *supposed* to fall, suffer confusion or pain, leak urine, lose interest in life, or change in any other significant way.

Age is not a disease. However, it is real. Changes do occur with aging and may mean that a senior will need to change the way they participate in some activities. It does not mean they have to stop.

✳✳✳✳✳✳✳✳✳✳✳✳✳✳✳✳✳✳✳✳✳✳✳✳✳

 This is my ninety-four-year-old Aunt Terri. She taught advanced line-dancing classes three days per week until she decided that hearing loss interfered with her teaching. Since then, she has taught the basic steps in an occasional introductory class; she dances with the group at events, helps plan excursions for her senior center, and travels somewhere every couple of months. She also fends off advances from men twenty years younger.

A few years ago, my Aunt Terri flew from Philadelphia, PA to Chicago to join me for Friends and Family Weekend at my church. She danced everybody off the floor (and even brought her own music in case we didn't have the sounds she loved.) I haven't been able to get her back out here because I can't get on her calendar to compete with a Mediterranean cruise, trip to the Grand Canyon, or local concerts, lectures, movies, and plays.

I want to be Aunt Terri when I grow up! She is living proof that age is not a disease. Even though she did not feel she could teach dancing at her previous level, Aunt Terri found a way to continue to do what she loves on her own terms.

✳✳✳✳✳✳✳✳✳✳✳✳✳✳✳✳✳✳✳✳✳✳✳✳✳

My former pastor, Rev. Dr. Frank Thomas explained it this way: "A young basketball player drives to the hoop; when he gets older, he develops a fade-away jump shot. He still scores."

Remember, changes in a senior's behavior are *never* due to aging alone. Don't give up and accept disability without looking for a condition that health professionals can treat. If cure isn't possible, there may be ways to make it easier for the senior to participate in her usual activities, or make other changes that might support his joy and quality of life. It's up to the caregiver to recognize and face problems and ask for tests and accommodations.

In 2017, the Mayo Clinic website presented eight questions for care-givers to ask when they wondered whether an older adult was at risk.[14]. Are your aging parents:

- Taking care of themselves?
- Experiencing memory loss?
- Safe in their homes?
- Safe on the road?
- Losing weight?
- In good spirits?
- Still social?
- Able to get around?

I would expand the first question.

- Have they changed the way they attend to hygiene or housekeeping?
- Is there enough food in the house? Is it spoiled? Are there burned pots?
- Have they lost interest in activities they used to enjoy or are they less capable in activities they had done well?)

I would also add another warning sign. Changes in financial management should raise concern. For example, one senior spent $25,000 on electric beds. Another previously astute businessman spent $12,000 on packing materials yet failed to pay his quarterly business taxes. Other elders purchase thousands of dollars of "stuff" from online advertisers and have trouble paying rent. Many seniors become victims of online or telephone scammers and other financial predators. Find out whether your aging relatives have financial problems. Ask:

- Does he pay bills late or forget to pay bills altogether?
- Does she spend large amounts of money on strange purchases?
- Is he contributing to a lot of "charities?"
- Are strange people calling or hanging around?
- Does she seem to run out of necessities, or ask you for money?

*Don't deny* that your senior might have a problem. No matter how scary it is, how much it hurts, and no matter who raises the possibility (even your bossy brother or your spoiled sister), check it out.

*Don't give in to ageism.* Don't convince yourself or accept anyone's opinion that the changes you see are "just old age" (don't believe that even from a doctor.)

### Don't Delay. Dare to be Direct.

Denial and ageism will make you miss opportunities to help your senior. They also cause families to delay interventions until there is an accident, illness, or other emergency.

If you see or hear of a problem with a senior, *don't wait*; investigate immediately. Delay may let a condition worsen until there is no chance for improvement or cure. Of course, investigation might confirm your worst fear; the condition may not be curable, but if you drag your feet, you won't be able to ease suffering or plan for excellent care over time.

Some families are reluctant to impose on an elder, to offend, or interfere in her affairs. They should ask themselves: *Is it worse to make the senior angry, or to deal with guilt because you let something happen to him?*

\*\*\*\*\*\*\*\*\*\*\*\*\*\*\*\*\*\*\*\*\*\*\*\*\*\*

Mr. Riegel's family was increasingly concerned about his driving because he often drove twenty miles per hour in a fifty-five mile per hour zone. He also straddled the line that separated him from oncoming traffic and forgot directions to familiar places. Mr. Riegel's daughter, Karyn, did not want to "limit Dad's independence." She insisted, "He only drives in the neighborhood and to his sister's house."

One Sunday afternoon, Mr. Riegel's sister called Karyn to report that he had never arrived for dinner. There was no answer at his home. No one had heard from him and according to the pastor, no one had seen him after church.

Karyn searched the neighborhood well into the evening. She was frantic by 9 p.m. when she received a call from the police in a town over 200 miles away. A large water pipe had ruptured on the street Mr. Riegel usually travelled from the church to his sister's house, and the fire department erected barriers to redirect drivers. When Mr. Riegel turned to take the short detour, he could not figure out how to get back on the right route. He drove until he was out of gas and walked away from his car. The police found him wandering down the interstate highway, frightened, agitated, and confused.

\*\*\*\*\*\*\*\*\*\*\*\*\*\*\*\*\*\*\*\*\*\*\*\*\*\*

This story and others in the previous discussion on denial show the dangers of delayed attention to changes in a senior's abilities.

- Mr. Riegel's daughter did not address her father's driving problems because she did not want to "offend" him. Instead, her reluctance endangered him. He was lucky that a car did not hit him and that he did not encounter a mugger. Mr. Riegel was also lucky that the episode happened in the spring. Dehydration in extreme heat or hypothermia (low body temperature) and frostbite in cold weather could have spelled disaster.

- Mrs. Miller's son ignored her friends' warnings until he came home to find that home invaders had victimized his mother. Mrs. Miller raised a successful man. She must have helped her son with his grade school projects. Did he think his mother had *never* known about magic markers? If Robert Miller had been willing to consider that Mrs. Miller's friends might have valid concerns, he might have intervened in time to protect his mother from physical and financial harm. Instead, like many other adult children, he was not open to the possibility that his parent was not the person she had been. He did *nothing,* and the outcome was both dangerous and sad.

- Neither Mrs. Reese's family, her primary care doctor, nor even Mrs. Reese herself, understood that the problem with her knee was not normal aging. If they had, she might have participated in physical therapy before the pain made her stop dancing. Instead, Mrs. Reese gave up an activity that brought her joy. She descended into depression, felt hopeless, and stopped moving at all. Decreased activity triggered the blood clot and a cascade of health problems that could have caused permanent disability or death.

## Remember...

**Don't deny**. If you or anyone else has a concern about your senior's health or behavior, investigate and get help right away.

**Don't delay**. Instead of missing chances to protect your senior, grab those opportunities with both hands. That's the way to avoid injury, relieve suffering, and plan for the best care. Move to preserve your senior's quality of life NOW!

*But don't despair. You don't have to face this alone.*

# CHAPTER 4

# Don't Despair: There Is Help
*Find Out What You Need to Do*

**Use the Emergency Room for** *Emergencies*

Whether due to denial, unresolved fighting, or lack of awareness, many families don't get help for an ailing senior until there is an emergency. Unfortunately, this is the least efficient way to get the help an elder needs.

The emergency room is for *medical emergencies* that pose *immediate* danger to life and limb. These may include heart attacks, strokes, serious infections and injuries, uncontrolled bleeding, diarrhea, pain, or vomiting, severe dehydration, problems breathing, or walking, and *sudden* changes in behavior and thinking. The emergency room is not intended to address *life emergencies* in which caregivers just discovered a chronic condition. Neither are emergency rooms the place to go when ongoing care needs overwhelm caregiving resources.

In my medical practice, I saw families leave seniors at the emergency room when the caregiver became incapacitated (due to an illness or injury,) or she had a sudden increase in duties (for example, assuming responsibility for someone's children or another older adult). I have even seen families do this as a matter of convenience when the caregiver planned a vacation.

Either way, this is inappropriate, and it doesn't work.

Many families believe they can drop a senior off at the emergency room; the person can stay in the hospital for a couple of days, go to a nursing home, and Medicare will pay for everything. *This is not true* though many first responders, attorneys, and even some social service professionals continue to counsel families to do this.

If the senior does not have a medical condition (like a heart attack, stroke, serious operation, infection, or injury) that requires acute inpatient hospital care for at least two midnights, Medicare will classify the hospital stay as either "observation" or "outpatient in a bed." The Medicare nursing home benefit does not apply to these days in the hospital. Since Medicare Part A covers neither "observation" nor "outpatient in a bed," the senior is responsible for the Medicare Part B copayment of twenty percent of every doctor visit, medicine, test, and treatment. (*See Chapter 17: Paying for Eldercare*, which discusses Medicare financing in greater detail).

These emergency room drop-offs can cost seniors and their families thousands of dollars. They can also expose the senior to healthcare-associated infections, and other hospital risks. Instead of running to the emergency room, be proactive and look for caregiving support options before you become overwhelmed. Many community-based professionals and resources are available to help caregivers. This help comes from a comprehensive geriatrics assessment, what I call the Level of Care Prescription (LOCRx,) the family conference, social service professionals, and the resources of other community programs.

### Get a Comprehensive Geriatrics Assessment

The geriatrics assessment goes beyond the basic medical examination, which investigates physical symptoms to diagnose and treat illness. The goal of the geriatrics assessment is also to recommend ways to protect independence and quality of life. Unique aspects of this examination include tests of:

FUNCTION

Specially trained health professionals measure a senior's ability to see and hear, and her mobility (walking, navigating stairs, getting in and out of bed, chairs, and cars, and other activities). They also test nutrition and the ability to control the bowels and bladder. By interviewing the family and sometimes visiting the home, team members learn what the person must do to live safely in that environment. This assessment allows professionals to recommend ways to bridge the gap between what the senior *can* do and what she *needs* to do to take care of herself. Recommendations may include treatments to improve the senior's medical condition, therapy to strengthen muscles, assistive devices (like canes, walkers, and special utensils), or changes to the home (like grab bars, lifts, or ramps).

## COGNITIVE AND BEHAVIORAL HEALTH

Another unique aspect of the geriatrics assessment tests brain function (cognition) and looks for mental health conditions including depression. There are simple tests of mood, short-term memory, who and where you are, the date, time, and current events (orientation). Other tests show how the senior uses and understands language. There are also tests of visuospatial skills (the ability to see in three dimensions, judge how close objects are to each other, and recognize where one object begins and another ends). If the test results are normal or inconclusive, and the senior or family still has concerns about brain function, the team can call in neuropsychologists. There are PhDs who specialize in many aspects of brain function, including learning disorders, brain injuries, and illnesses that affect memory and complex decision-making. The team can consult geriatric psychiatrists who specialize in mental health concerns of the elderly. They can also consult neurologists who are expert in diseases of the brain and nervous system. These professionals can provide more in-depth testing and make recommendations about care plans.

## MEDICINE REVIEW

The goal of this service is to ensure that all medicines are necessary and in the right doses for the older adult's system ("gero-friendly"). The medicine review is important because a study showed that problems with medicines were the eighth most common reason for seniors to go into hospitals.[15] Geriatrics professionals use the term *polypharmacy* to describe the overuse and possible misuse of medicines, which can lead to overdose, confusion, falls, and other serious side effects. Polypharmacy also puts seniors at risk for dangerous interactions between prescription medicines. There may also be dangerous interactions with over-the-counter drugs, food, vitamins, and other nutritional supplements.

Polypharmacy often occurs because a senior may see several doctors: the primary care physician, surgeons, and several consultants for ailments of the heart, lungs, joints, or other organ systems. Each doctor may write prescriptions and if they do not communicate with each other, the senior may take many medicines for the same condition, or different doses of the same medicine.

The professionals address possible polypharmacy by performing a

"Brown Bag" test. They ask the family to empty the medicine cabinets, furniture drawers, and any other possible hiding places to collect *every* medicine bottle and bring them to the visit in a bag (brown or any other color). This review determines whether any of the drugs are responsible for the senior's symptoms either alone or by interaction with other chemicals. Health professional want to separate past prescriptions, expired, duplicate, and unnecessary drugs from the ones they want the senior to take. They also decide whether to adjust the doses or timing of the necessary medicines.

The health care team will develop a medicine list. They will also teach caregivers to recognize each medicine, understand why the senior needs it, and know the proper dose and the correct dosing schedule. They will also give instructions about whether the senior should take the medicine with or without food, with other medicines or at different times, and how to check for side effects.

## CAREGIVING RESOURCES

Once the care needs are clear, additional questions address the wishes and values of the senior and his family, the location where they want the care to take place, and the resources available to them. Important factors include: enough time and support from family members or other helpers, finances, and the availability of a living space that is safe and easy for the patient to use. It is equally important to consider the senior's and caregiver's beliefs, attitudes, and ability to cope.

Developing an effective and workable care plan goes beyond the skills of any one type of professional. Experts from several professions (or disciplines) form a team to conduct the assessments and design the care plan. This is called the *multi-disciplinary team.*

### Who's on the Multi-Disciplinary Geriatrics Team?

## GERIATRICIANS

Geriatricians are doctors who train in Internal Medicine (healthcare for adults) or Family Medicine before choosing to spend at least one more year concentrating on the care of seniors. Geriatrics is a full subspecialty, like Cardiology (heart problems) or Gastroenterology (diseases of the stomach, bowels, and liver). Geriatricians are "board certified," like doctors in these other subspecialties.

**BEWARE!** I have met doctors who add the words *geriatrics* or *gerontology* to their business cards and other official papers. They hope to attract Baby Boomers (many of whom value designer labels) and portray themselves as "designer doctors." Remember, geriatrics is a subspecialty that requires specific training and expertise.

*Having older adults in the practice does not make a doctor a geriatrician any more than having patients with hearts makes the doctor a cardiologist.*

Also, the terms "gerontologist" and "geriatrician" are not interchangeable. Gerontology is the *study* of aging. Geriatrics is the *practice* of providing healthcare and other services to older adults. The primary focus is frail seniors who are at risk of nursing home placement. A gerontologist usually does research. A geriatrician provides patient care.

*A doctor can be both; a doctor can be either, but a doctor who offers full-time direct care services, does no research, and advertises as a gerontologist is probably neither!*

Review your state's board of professional licensing and regulations to be sure the doctor you choose has training and board certification in Geriatric Medicine.

## MORE GERIATRICS TEAM MEMBERS

The team may also include:

- Advance practice professionals (nurse practitioners [NP] or physician assistants [PA]) with special training in geriatrics.
- Behavioral health professionals (neurobehavioral specialists, psychiatrists, psychologists)
- Neurologists.
- Nurses.
- Nutritionists.
- Pharmacists.
- Occupational, Physical, and Speech Therapists.
- Social Workers.

Team members may also consult physiatrists (doctors who specialize in Physical Medicine and Rehabilitation [PM&R]) surgeons, and other specialists (like cardiologists), depending on the senior's health challenges.

In my mind, a geriatrics "dream team" would also include vocational rehabilitation specialists (to help seniors get back to work if possible), elder law attorneys, financial/estate planners, realtors, and tax professionals to assist with:

- Wills, designating alternate decision-makers for healthcare, finance, and guardianship.

- Transfer or sale of property.
- Trusts and tax planning.

### How Do You Find a Multi-Disciplinary Geriatrics Team?

University hospitals and Geriatric Medicine training programs usually offer geriatrics assessments. Information may also be available from local area agencies on aging, state and local medical societies, departments on aging, and geriatrics societies. You can also contact health system physician-referral telephone lines, home health agencies, and hospice programs. AARP, the American Geriatrics Society (AGS), and the American Medical Association (AMA) are also resources for finding a geriatrics team.

You may be able to find a team through lawyers, bankers, realtors, and other professionals who serve an older adult clientele. This is especially true in urban and suburban communities where the eldercare network is strong and well-coordinated. Rural communities may have fewer resources.

Sadly, it is hard to find a geriatrics team anywhere (*See Chapter 19: Is There a Doctor in the House? Why Aren't There Enough Geriatricians*). If you cannot find a program that includes all the necessary professionals in one place, you can contact the professionals individually. Health system and health insurance company provider information phonelines and websites will help locate individual professionals as well as teams. State departments on aging, the Area Agency on Aging, and faith-based programs are good places to get information about social service team members. Most local pharmacists will review medicines with you without charge though you may have to schedule an appointment.

### What Should You Bring to the Appointment?

*Bernie Ryan's Healthcare Information Binder*

Make the most of your time with any doctor or care team by being as organized as possible. Back in the 1990s, Ms. Bernie Ryan taught me an effective way to do this. The Ryans are a large, Irish-Catholic family with several adult children spread around the country; one lives in Ireland. Bernie was their parents' primary caregiver. You can imagine the possible communication problems, but Bernie had a foolproof system. She prepared a three-ring binder with divider tabs like the ones students carry. Each tab identified a specific topic and provided a place to store related documents. Today, the tech-savvy can keep this information on a smartphone or tablet. Whether you prefer paper or digital record-keeping, these are Bernie's dividers with my explanations and other recommendations I've made over the years.

1) *Contact information for all professionals.* This section includes doctors, home health agencies, outpatient health services, preferred pharmacies, and community services. Include a signed letter with contact information for family members and anyone else the senior wants to have access to their health information.

2) *Medical history* list of current and past conditions. Don't forget pregnancies, surgeries, other procedures, hospital visits, and allergies.

3) *List of medicines.* If your health team does not send prescriptions to the pharmacy electronically, this is a good place to keep prescriptions. In the next section of this chapter, *What Should You Bring to the Appointment,* you will see a picture of the form I developed to record all information about your senior's medicines. You can also get a copy by visiting my website: www.drcherylwoodson.com.

4) *Insurance information.* In this section, keep insurance cards, letters from insurance companies that confirm approval or denial of services, as well as referrals and orders for tests or procedures.

5) *Legal documents.* These include Advance Directives: Living Will, Powers of Attorney, and POLST (for a description of this advance directive, see *Chapter 16: End of Life Care: Adding Life to Years, Not Just Life to Years*). This section should also include guardianship and disability documents.

6) *Communications.* Here, Bernie kept blank paper for organizing thoughts, information, and questions before the visit. In addition to recording her questions as they arose between visits, Bernie often canvassed her siblings and presented comments and concerns from the family members who could not come to the appointment. She also wrote down answers and instructions.

I added two sections.

7) *Test Results.* Keep results of blood tests, x-rays and other procedures. This is especially important if a doctor other than your primary care physician (PCP) ordered the tests. Ask the other doctors to send results to your PCP, but have this back-up plan.

8) *Appointment calendar.* Keep track of the senior's tests, appointments,

and activities. The caregiver should also record her work schedule, doctor appointments, other responsibilities (like parent-teacher conferences,) "me" time, and the availability of potential helpers.

Bernie made sure *the binder always moved with the seniors, no matter who brought them to the office.* This made things easier for everyone. The helpers could relieve Bernie, provide transportation, and not worry that they didn't have all the information about their parents' health or care plans. With the binder, Bernie didn't have to worry that any important issues would be overlooked. Helpers could also make follow-up appointments that did not conflict with Bernie's schedule. This avoided unnecessary calls to reschedule.

## The "Brown Bag" – Bring ALL Medicines in the House

This is the medicine management form I recommended in my practice. Request your copy from my website: www.drcherylwoodson.com.

### The Woodsonian Medicine Sheet

Page 1 of _____                                                                    Date _____

| Doctor's Name & Phone Number (for each pill) | MEDICINE Trade Name Chemical Name What's it for? How much? Refill Date | BREAKFAST | LUNCH | DINNER | BEDTIME |
|---|---|---|---|---|---|
| | <TAPE PILL> | <TAPE PILL> | <TAPE PILL> | <TAPE PILL> | <TAPE PILL> |
| Dr. Jones (PCP) (708) 555-1234 | Glucophage Metformin Diabetes 500mg 11/15/22 | XX (Before) | | X (Before) | |
| Dr. Smith (Kidney) (773) 555-5678 | Hyzaar Losaran-HCTZ BP, Kidneys 50/25 11/15/22 | X | | | |
| Dr. Brown (Heart) (708) 555-9101 | ECASA Coated Aspirin Prevent heart attack/stroke 81mg 11/15/22 | | X (With) | | |
| Dr. Brown (Heart) (708) 555-9101 | Lipitor Atorvastatin Cholesterol 20mg 11/15/22 | | | | X (with small snack) |

The form has six columns. The first column lists the name and phone number of the doctor who prescribed each pill. Caregivers should also record the doctor's specialty, for example, cardiology, or "heart doctor" because this adds another layer of information.

Drugs have a trade name used for advertising and a generic name that identifies the chemical. The second column of the medicine sheet lists the trade and the generic names of each medicine, the condition the medicine treats, the dose, and the next refill date.

Make the second column wide enough to tape a pill beside the name of each medicine. This helps if someone has problems with vision or reading. It also can avoid confusion when you refill a prescription, and the pill looks different. This happens because like you, pharmacies shop around for the best prices on medicines. They can change manufacturers every time they order supplies. Sometimes they change every month! Even though the pharmacy refills the same medicine in the same dose, the color, shape, or size of the pill may change.

\*\*\*\*\*\*\*\*\*\*\*\*\*\*\*\*\*\*\*\*\*\*\*\*\*\*\*\*\*\*

Eldercare consultant Melodee Leimnetzer handled prescription refills for a client. The pharmacy offered to fill one prescription with three different types of pills, because they did not have a full supply from one manufacturer. Luckily, Melodee had not waited until the last minute to request the refill; she was able to wait for the next shipment and get a full prescription with one type of pill. Even so, the new pills did not look like any of the client's previous prescriptions.

\*\*\*\*\*\*\*\*\*\*\*\*\*\*\*\*\*\*\*\*\*\*\*\*\*\*\*\*\*\*

I teach people not to identify their medicine by describing the pill. Even though you are used to taking "a little, square, blue pill," the next time you fill that prescription, the pill may not be little, square, or blue. Taping pills to the medicine chart will help avoid dangerous errors.

The Xs on the form indicate the time to give the medicine. The ( ) hold instructions about whether the senior should take the pill before, with, or after a meal. You can also use the ( ) to indicate how much time you should wait between the meal and the pill or before taking another pill in the same general time of day.

## Who Should Come to the Appointment?

Someone *must* accompany the senior to support him and help record information. For this first visit, it is best if this is the person who has the most contact with the older adult and/or the most information. It should not be the person who just happens to be available provide transportation that day. I understand that people have other commitments (Bernie Ryan's medical information binder is critical under those circumstances), but the initial evaluation lays the foundation for an effective care plan. For this first visit, the primary caregiver should try to be there.

Even when the main caregiver attends the first visit, it may be useful to have one other person present for an extra set of ears and another opportunity to understand information. When families have several involved relatives, office space cannot usually accommodate everyone in that first visit. Don't worry. Once the team has completed and reviewed the tests and reports from consultants, they can schedule a family meeting to explain the results to everyone. This meeting also starts the care planning process. (*See Chapter 4: Really Don't Despair – Social Service Professionals Help You Get the Job Done, - The Family Meeting*).

### *What If the Senior Refuses to Keep the Appointment?*

Many older adults refuse doctor visits because they don't think they need help. Even if they know something is amiss, some seniors aren't happy that other people think so. Resistance can also cover fear.

When you make the appointment, ask the team for recommendations about handling resistance. My staff and I used several effective strategies to encourage seniors' cooperation. A reluctant older adult may agree to a comprehensive geriatrics assessment if a trusted primary care clinician (PCP, nurse practitioner, or physician's assistant) recommends the visit. When the PCP says, "I need some information from a specialist," the senior may see the geriatrics professionals as consultants who work with (or for) the PCP. This extends the mantle of trust and credibility from the PCP to the geriatrics team.

Other seniors may feel less threatened if a spouse, friend, or adult child suggests they both "get a checkup." As a last resort, I have recommended that families take the senior out for a meal or another fun activity, and end up at the geriatrics site. Geriatrics teams are expert at putting seniors at ease and getting their cooperation. Team members have specific training in diffusing tension and overcoming resistance. They can often turn resentment to curiosity or at least grudging cooperation. The key is to treat the senior with respect, try to make the experience fun, and be flexible.

Many seniors have chosen to cooperate when I thanked them for giving me an opportunity to see "a healthy older adult." When I worked with medical students, I often won a reluctant senior over when I asked her to "help me teach these young doctors the proper respect for older people." (I also insisted my students send "thank-you" notes to every person they served!) Although I found that these strategies put the geriatrics assessment in a more positive light, it did not always work. Once I had to complete a geriatrics assessment while walking a senior around my parking lot.

## *What Will Happen During the Appointment?*

If all team members are in the same program, the assessment can take place in one appointment that lasts for several hours. There are also "virtual teams" where the members work in different offices, share information, and coordinate services in a community network. Virtual team assessments can take two to three weeks and typically include several forty-five to ninety-minute sessions.

Following the first visit, the geriatrics team usually orders blood tests and/or X-rays to confirm or clarify problems found in that visit. The team may also refer the senior to specialists when specific body systems are at risk. For example, team members may consult a cardiologist when they suspect a heart problem. The consultants may order more intensive tests that refine the team's approach to the senior's needs.

## *What Will the Team Ask You?*

In addition to the medical history, the team will ask:
- What problems does the family see?
- When did the problems begin?
- How have they changed over time?
- What makes them worse or better (certain activities, times of day, people, changes in the environment, other factors)?
- What specific tasks can the older adult perform well? What activities are difficult for him?

## *What Should You Ask the Team?*

In the first edition, I presented the "Ask Me 3" program that the National Patient Safety Foundation developed to help people understand their healthcare plans.[16]
- What is my main problem?

- What do I need to do?

- Why is it important for me to do this?

Though I still find Ask Me 3 easy for caregivers, I believe it is useful to add questions that clarify the timeline and the consequences of not following the plan.

- How much time do I have to get this done?

- If there are several instructions, what should I do first, second, and so on?

- What happens if I *don't* follow the instructions?

*Ask for Written Instructions*

Even when you take notes or have an extra person to hear the team's recommendations, you will have questions once you get home. When you have this information in writing, you avoid delays from playing phone tag with the geriatrics team. This will also avoid emergencies, and prevent unnecessary trips to the hospital.

The instructions should include:

- An updated medicine list that describes any new medicines, changes in the doses of current medicines, instructions about how to use medicines safely, and which medicines the senior should not take at all.

- A description of signs and symptoms that suggest your loved one's condition is getting worse. For example:

  - What are acceptable ranges for blood sugar, blood pressure, weight, temperature, the number of heart beats or breaths per minute?

  - How often should you take these measurements?

  - At what point should you call the doctor? When should you go to the emergency room?

- Referral forms for tests and consultations with other professionals

- Instructions for follow-up appointments

- What should you do if you have more questions?

- Does the practice use email or programs like MyChart?

- What is the best time of day to call and which team member is the point person?

- After I call, when should I expect answers?

The team will usually schedule the follow up appointment within a few weeks. It can be sooner if the elder's condition needs urgent treatment or later if the team must gather and review test results and notes from consultants. At that appointment, they will discuss their findings and present what I call the Level of Care Prescription (LOCRx™).

## The Level of Care Prescription (LOCRx)

Many caregivers say they feel like they are running in circles. Though they do everything they can, they worry about doing enough, doing the right things, and missing important care needs. Worry causes fear, guilt, and stress.

The difference between what the senior *can* do and what she *needs* to do to be independent is the **Level of Care.** Geriatrics teams *prescribe* the level of care. The LOCRx rescues caregivers from doubt by providing specific information that empowers them to move forward with confidence.

The geriatrics team develops the LOCRx by answering ten questions. The first five define the problem.

1) **What is wrong with the senior?**

2) **Why is it wrong?**

3) **How much of what's wrong is fixable?**

4) **How can we fix that part?**

5) **How can we manage the part we cannot fix?**

The next five questions outline the care plan.

6) **What kind of care does the senior need?**
   Is it enough for her grandson to cut the grass once a week, or does she need hands-on care for pressure sores (bed sores)?

7) **How much care does the person need?**
   If there are pressure sores, is it enough to change his position every two hours to prevent new sores, or does the caregiver need to clean and treat deep wounds?

8) **How often does the senior need this care?**

If the challenge is wound care, how often should the caregiver clean the wounds and change the dressings: three times a day, once a day, every three days?

**9) How long will the person need this care?**
By giving careless answers to this ninth question, physicians fail families. Only God knows the length of the caregiving season. Doctors don't know how long an illness will last and we cannot give accurate predictions about how long a person will need care. Doctors do know whether we can cure the condition with a shot of antibiotics or if the family can expect a senior's care needs to increase or decrease, over time. Arbitrary estimates give false hope and create unrealistic expectations that can blindside families as reality unfolds.

Instead of subjective timelines, doctors should outline the most common course of the illness with clear descriptions of factors that can change that process for the individual. For example, instead of telling a family that a certain condition will last for a specific amount of time, doctors should say, "Though some people live with W (condition) for X (amount of time), your father also has other dangerous problems, Y and Z, that make this less likely for him. There is no way to know exactly how things will move along, but if we see (specific symptoms, test results, and signs of improving or worsening illness), we will know it is time to change the treatment plan like this (possible next steps)." As the test results reveal how the senior's condition is moving, the discussion should also include possible care needs going forward (full recovery right away, at home with help or a care facility for a slower recovery, or chronic disability with long-term care needs). This approach also gives clear signals that can help the family prepare for the time when all treatment options have been exhausted. If they have had the opportunity to think about this in advance, it may be easier to open discussions about hospice care. (See *Chapter 16: End-of-Life Care: Adding Life to Years, Not Just Years to Life*).

Unclear timetables also make families try to provide care at home with one or two people when three shifts of nurses deliver the same care in a nursing facility. Although families might be able to manage complicated care plans for a few weeks or even several months, can they do it several *years?* Specific milestones that allow more realistic expectations not only avoid the pain of dashed hopes but also prevent caregiver burnout. If families understand that their care responsibilities will continue (or increase) for the rest of the senior's life, they are less likely to underestimate the amount of help they need, or overestimate how long they can hang on.

The final LOCRx question is:

**10) How much education should the caregiver have?**
Does the senior just need her granddaughter (who has no medical background) to write out bills twice a month, or does the elder have complicated care needs that require a registered nurse twenty-four hours per day, seven days per week?

LOCRx is a Woodsonism, a term I created. Even though your geriatrics team may not call their report the LOCRx, the information they present will include the answers to these ten essential questions.

Once the geriatrics team develops the LOCRx, social service professionals help seniors and their families review their resources and clarify their values. With this information, families can decide how and where caregivers can provide the care.

## The Difference Between Level of Care and Locus of Care

The *level* of care is the intensity of care your loved one needs and the necessary type of caregiver training. The *locus* of care is the most appropriate place to give that care. While the locus of care decision requires a thorough understanding of the level of care, they are separate decisions. The locus of care also considers the values of the senior and his family, their personal and financial resources, and the services available in the community they choose.

For example, someone who needs round-the-clock supervision does not always require a nursing home if she has enough family support or enough money to hire the necessary in-home help. A person who does not have family support may still be able to avoid a nursing home if he qualifies for assisted living. He must not need daily or even frequent medical care. He must be able to walk or use a cane, walker, or wheelchair to get to the dining room. He has to do this and be able to leave the building with little or no help. The person must also be able to afford to live in the facility (with or without a government subsidy).

The locus of care will differ based on changes in the person's health status, their wishes, and resources over time. With every change, social service professionals help families find appropriate care sites.

# CHAPTER 5

## Really! Don't Despair: *Social Service Professionals Help You Do the Job*

These professionals find the safest care site using the LOCRx, family values, resources, and what is available in the community. They also find out if the senior meets requirements for state-subsidized services, and they provide caregivers with ongoing information and support. These professionals are also experienced in managing the family conflict these discussions can reveal.

### The Family Conference: *Professionals at Work; Don't Try This at Home*

Most geriatrics teams host a conference to present the LOCRx and answer questions from the senior and family. Social service team members spend additional time to determine the locus of care. This may also happen in a separate meeting.

Although family conferences are usually helpful, they can also dredge up old resentments and deteriorate into shouting matches that fail the older adult. This also places an extra burden on an already overwhelmed caregiver and leaves scars on family relationships that cause pain long after the senior dies.

The person who runs the conference must be an objective referee who doesn't care which child was Mom's favorite or to whom Dad gave a car in high school. This person must also have expertise and credibility to move conflicts aside and keep the focus on the common goal: to give the senior the best care.

Many caregiver resources recommend that a respected family member should serve in this role. In my experience, the family member with enough clout to control the situation is the one who's sick. When Grandma was healthy, she gave marching orders, and everybody fell in line. Chaos reigns when Grandma cannot use her influence to stabilize the situation, either because of her own illness or because she's upset by Grandpa's health problems.

Social service professionals are excellent facilitators. They have experience in the illnesses of aging and understand the LOCRx. They are knowledgeable about eldercare resources and skilled in managing family dynamics. Geriatricians, primary care doctors, eldercare consultants, and advance practice professionals (nurse practitioners and physician assistants) are good choices for this role. Psychiatrists, psychologists, and clergy can also be very effective.

The facilitator takes the heat for introducing touchy topics like limits on driving and other activities, nursing home placement, and decisions about care at the end of life. These professionals are also responsible to support and protect the caregiver. They control blame-laying, name-calling, and other counter-productive behaviors. They also become the bearer of bad news to spare the caregiver; the baby sister isn't telling older siblings what to do; the professionals *prescribe* the plan of action. In over thirty years of facilitating these meetings, I have prevented several fights and had to call the police only once.

The team should invite every interested family member to the conference. (As I said, I invited people who could not attend the meeting to join by conference call.) This way, everyone hears the information at the same time; all family members have an opportunity to voice their concerns and ask questions. This eliminates the "he said, she said" that leads to misinformation, misunderstandings, and further conflict. The team can document any commitments family members make and pave the way for accountability (See *Chapter 8: Get Help from Family and Friends, - Show Up or Shut Up*).

Darby J. Morhardt, PhD, is my good friend and an Associate Professor at the Mesulam Center for Cognitive Neurology and Alzheimer's Disease at Northwestern University's Feinberg School of Medicine in Chicago, Illinois. In addition to being an accomplished researcher and educator, she is masterful in supporting caregivers and helping families with care planning.

Early in our careers, Dr. Morhardt and I worked together in the Geriatric Evaluation Service at Northwestern Memorial Hospital; she was the social worker, and I was one of the primary care geriatricians. We co-facilitated many conferences, including one that involved a large, volatile family.

＊＊＊＊＊＊＊＊＊＊＊＊＊＊＊＊＊＊＊＊＊＊＊＊＊＊

The primary caregiver was the youngest sister, a high school graduate, and file clerk. She was overwhelmed by caregiving yet felt outranked by her older siblings who had advanced degrees and professional careers. They came to the meeting armed with Internet research and berated their baby sister about suggesting nursing home placement for their grandmother when the LOCRx recommended twenty-four-hour care. Although several of them lived out of town, they all claimed they would pitch in to care for Grandmom at home.

Dr. Morhardt asked whether the family members wanted to work in two-, three-, or four-hour shifts each day and asked for specific time commitments from each one: "Who will take eight a.m. to noon, noon to four p.m.," and so on. Everyone agreed to cover a shift, run errands, assume other responsibilities, or contribute funds to hire a worker when they were not available. Dr. Morhardt made a chart to document commitments that covered twenty-four hours and gave everyone a copy of the schedule. The family agreed to review the plan in one month.

By the second week, scheduled family members had not shown up. Some had cancelled at the last minute, leaving several shifts uncovered. They balked when the primary caregiver asked them to pick up groceries or take her children to school, and no one provided any money. The primary caregiver had to take unpaid leave from work while also paying workers to fill in any gaps until she could arrange nursing home placement.

＊＊＊＊＊＊＊＊＊＊＊＊＊＊＊＊＊＊＊＊＊＊＊＊＊

If your geriatrics service does not have a social worker, it will provide referrals and contact information for community social service professionals.

## Professional Eldercare Consultants

These are usually social workers or nurses whom families hire privately. One way to locate eldercare consultants in your area is through the Aging Life Care Association (formerly the National Association of Professional Geriatric Care Managers). The website (www.aginglifecare.org) provides lists of eldercare consultants by the zip code of the senior who needs care. Every professional whose information appears on the website has undergone a certification process.

Eldercare consultants are excellent resources for finding geriatricians, educating and supporting caregivers, investigating care options, and addressing family conflict. These specialists can also make home visits to begin the examination for seniors who either cannot come to an office visit or refuse to do so. The consultants can hire and supervise in-home workers, take seniors to doctor visits, and serve as information bridges between doctors and families. These professionals can be a Godsend, especially for working and long-distance caregivers.

Eldercare consultants also identify care resources appropriate to the specific situation. They communicate with service providers and help families prepare applications. They also cut "red tape" and ensure that caregivers do not waste time applying for services that do not match the seniors' needs, values, or finances.

The fees for these services differ by state. Whatever cost you encounter, don't panic. Eldercare consultants do not provide direct care. They coordinate care and after the initial assessment, typically spend only a few hours a month to monitor and update the plan. In some cases, family members chip in to share the cost. This is the best money a family can spend.

Some long-term care insurance policies cover these services. However, Medicare, public aid, and most other health insurance plans do not. Some state-funded agencies have case management units that set fees on a sliding scale, based on the senior's income (*not yours*). They offer some of the services that private eldercare consultants provide.

As I said, professional eldercare consultants can be a Godsend for working or long-distance caregivers. In some cases, family members chip in to share the cost and it is the best money a family can spend.


## Community Care Programs

State-funded agencies provide eldercare services through local departments on aging and area agencies on aging. These organizations use a Determination of Need (DON) score to assign services based on a senior's needs. Most calculate fees and copayments on a sliding scale, based on the senior's income.

These programs do not offer skilled nursing care, and Medicare and other health insurance plans do not pay for these services. Community care workers provide support services in the home. These include:

- Companionship
- Housekeeping
- Laundry
- Meal preparation
- Personal care
- Transportation

Although these helpers cannot give medicine, they can remind seniors what to take and when.

Some programs train specific workers to assist with bill-paying by completing forms, writing out checks for the senior to sign, and keeping records. To avoid financial exploitation, families must investigate these programs carefully and pay close attention to financial records.

## Assisted-Living Facilities

These residential communities offer housekeeping, meals, activities, transportation, and limited supervision. Facilities accept people with canes, walkers, wheelchairs, electric chairs, and scooters. However, residents must be able to get to the dining area and out of the building on their own or with assistance from an aide. Apartments have call systems so seniors can alert the staff if they need help. Employees also check on residents daily and stop in more often if the resident stops participating in activities or misses several meals.

Some facilities allow families to pay for extra help with personal care and managing medicines. People who need nursing care are supposedly ineligible for admission to these residences. However, home health agencies often affiliate with them and provide Medicare-certified skilled nursing services on site, under a physician's order. Unless the facility specifies dementia-care, the regulations exclude people whose primary disability is dementia. (*See Chapter 18: Assisted-Living Facilities*).

### Respite Services

Every caregiver needs a break. City- and state-supported respite workers can come into the home for a few hours each week and some can stay over a weekend. Assisted-living facilities and nursing homes provide longer-term respite (usually one to two weeks), when a caregiver is sick, needs surgery, or plans a vacation. In-patient hospice units offer short-term respite (several days) for families that support people within incurable conditions at home. Some health or long-term care insurance plans may cover the cost of these services, but Medicare and Medicaid do not. Many faith-based programs provide volunteers to sit with a senior for a few hours for free.

### Senior Centers

Relatively healthy seniors can take advantage of state-supported centers or similar programs offered by civic organizations that may include the Veterans of Foreign Wars (VFW), Masonic lodges, and faith-based programs. These centers offer non-medical services that include:

- Book clubs, seminars and discussion groups
- Crafts
- Exercise
- Games
- Meals
- Movies
- Outings to shopping malls and other places of interest
- Socialization
- Transportation

Many centers also serve as drop-in lunch programs and cooling or warming centers during inclement weather.

### Private Case Management Companies

A growing number of private companies perform the dual role of recommending care resources while providing the same direct-care services as the community care programs. Many also supply private-duty nurses and will help seniors find appropriate housing. Although private services do not have the long waiting lists that can plague state-funded programs, increased access usually comes with higher cost. Again, Medicare and Medicaid do not help with these services, though some long-term care insurance plans may.

## Adult Day Centers

Adult day centers are helpful for working caregivers and for anyone who needs a break, if only for a few half-days per week. Some centers allow intermittent drop-in services rather than long-term contracts. Others offer evening and weekend hours. Most centers are privately owned and charge families directly, while some accept state subsidies and use a sliding fee-scale based on the senior's income.

Like the community care programs, these centers provide support services.

- Baths
- Crafts and games
- Discussions of current events and other topics of interest
- Medication management
- Outings, and physical activity.
- Social interaction and discussions
- Transportation.

Some adult day centers allow home health agencies (nurses and therapists) to visit seniors to give limited care onsite.

## Faith-based Eldercare Resources

Houses of worship have begun to join forces with area agencies on aging, Alzheimer's research centers, and geriatrics programs to support caregivers. An example of this partnership is Research and Education for African-American Caregiver Health (REACH). This ecumenical, southside Chicago coalition involves Beth Eden Baptist Church, Covenant United Church of Christ, Fernwood, Lily Dale, St. Sabina Catholic Church, Trinity United Church of Christ, the Endeleo Institute (a community development organization), and the Mesulam Center for Cognitive Neurology and Alzheimer's Disease at Northwestern University. REACH plans to develop resource libraries in each church and has participated in dementia-friendly programs and caregiver support services at the Carter G. Woodson Regional Library.

The house of worship usually hears the first cries for help. All congregations can support caregivers with by offering educational programs, support groups and resource libraries. I hope national, regional, and local governing bodies of religious organizations will make it a priority to develop these resources and train clergy to support older members and their families.

In summary, to survive caregiving, you need to accept that your senior could have a problem (don't deny). You need to move quickly to learn what your senior needs (don't delay) and feel confident that there are certified experts to help you find appropriate resources (don't despair). Your survival kit includes comprehensive geriatrics assessment, the LOCRx, the family conference, professional eldercare consultants, and other private and community social service professionals to guide and support you.

Coordination between the primary care professionals, geriatrics teams, families, and social service professionals allows for close monitoring of the care plan and adjustments as the senior's health and care needs change. This can be difficult when caregivers have problems getting doctors to answer questions or when the answers don't make sense. There are ways to improve communication.

# CHAPTER 6

# The Physician User's Manual: *Get the Most from Your Doctors*

Caregiver stress can be fueled by frustration when families try to communicate with doctors. Effective communication can decrease stress for everyone. These recommendations apply not only to doctors but also to relationships other clinicians (health care professionals who offer direct health care services).

*************************

Mr. Gordon's daughter, Stephanie, was very angry with Dr. Hodges. She sat in her father's hospital room all day but never saw the doctor. She asked the nurses to call Dr. Hodges at the office. The office staff told the nurse the doctor was with another patient and could not come to the phone but would return the call at the end of the day. The receptionist left a message asking Dr. Hodges to call Mr. Gordon's "daughter." Mr. Gordon's oldest daughter, Marie, usually brought him to the office, and Dr. Hodges called her at 8pm. Marie did not know her sister had called the doctor and was unaware of Stephanie's concerns.

When Stephanie didn't hear from the doctor, she took another approach. The nurses had told her Dr. Hodges usually made rounds at 7 a.m. She informed the hospital security guard she was there to meet with the doctor and came up to the floor at 6:45 a.m. Dr. Hodges came in at 8:00 and since he had six patients to see in the hospital before starting his office hours at 9:30, he did not have time to answer all Stephanie's questions. She was livid. "That doctor made me come here for nothing," Stephanie said. "He breezed in here over an hour late and didn't even give me the time of day. He's not the only one who's busy; I have to work, too."

\*\*\*\*\*\*\*\*\*\*\*\*\*\*\*\*\*\*\*\*\*\*\*\*\*\*\*

This is a common miscommunication. The doctor's office did not realize they had the wrong daughter. The hospital staff did not know the doctor had a board meeting the next morning and planned to make rounds later than his usual time. No one had scheduled an appointment for Stephanie. Although this kind of communication is frustrating, there are more effective ways to connect.

### Communicate by Appointment, Not by Ambush

If you wanted to speak with your attorney, would you stand outside a courthouse and try to catch her as she rushed in to represent another client? Would you walk into a beauty salon and expect the stylist to stop serving the client in his chair to style your hair? No! In both instances, you would make an appointment. You would understand that without an appointment, the professional could not give you the time or service you needed. It's the same with doctors and other health care professionals.

Most doctors care for people in several sites every day: one or more hospitals, offices, and long-term care facilities. Some also make home visits. Even if you could "catch" the doctor at a care site, she has dedicated that time to serve the health needs of the people in that location. Rarely will she be able to stop and give you the time you need.

The same is true when you call and expect a doctor to come right to the phone (whether you call the office or sit at your senior's bedside and ask a nurse to call). If the doctor was giving care to your mother, would you want him to leave and take a non-emergency call from another family? Have the same consideration for the person under the doctor's care when you call to ask a routine question.

## Always Contact the Doctor Through the Office

No matter where the doctor cares for your loved one, you must call the doctor's *office* to make appointments and leave messages. Call the office, even if your loved one has never been there! You can ask nurses in hospitals, nursing homes, and other facilities to leave messages on your senior's chart, but the office is Control Central! Although the office staff may not have records from your loved one's care site, and they may not be able to answer your questions, calling the office is the best way to request and schedule a meeting with the doctor. While facility nurses may know when the doctor usually visits that site, only the office staff knows the doctor's entire schedule for a specific day. If the facility nurses seem uncomfortable about giving you the office number, you can find it on the Internet or through hospital and insurance company physician referral programs.

A doctor may work with advance practice professionals at hospitals and nursing homes. If those professionals keep offices in the facility, the nurses might be able to help you make a connection on site. Otherwise, contact them through the doctor's office as well.

## Can Someone Else Help You?

Caregivers often refuse to talk to receptionists, medical assistants, nurses, advance practice professionals, or office managers; either they don't respect these practice partners, or they worry about privacy. These caregivers fail to recognize the essential role of support personnel in a good medical practice.

Doctors design protocols to improve both communication and practice management. Advance practice professionals and office staff follow these protocols to answer your questions. For example, doctors do not usually handle appointment schedules, billing questions, requests for refills, referrals, and other paperwork. Instead of waiting to hear from the doctor, talk to the receptionist or nurse. Larger offices may have a clerk who is responsible for billing and insurance. In smaller offices, the office manager may answer these questions.

Medical assistants, nurses, and advance practice professionals usually handle questions about minor symptoms like itching, sneezing, and aches. They report normal test results, answer questions about medicines, and refill routine prescriptions. They can also get more timely answers to other questions by relaying them to the doctor on your behalf. If there are more serious medical concerns, they will follow the doctor's protocols to:

- Direct people with serious medical problems to the hospital or emergency department.

- Schedule people with less serious complaints or abnormal test results into special office appointments.

- Relay the doctor's standard orders about tests or consultations to guide common treatment decisions.

If the protocols don't address a specific situation, the staff will bring it to the doctor's immediate attention. Only calls that need instant medical decisions require a doctor to leave a sick person in an examination room to answer the phone.

### Tell the Staff *Exactly* What You Need

When you call the doctor's office, be as specific as possible. "I want to talk to the doctor" is *not* an effective message. The staff needs specific information to follow protocols and triage requests appropriately. Also remember *it's not first come, first served.* Doctors typically return non-emergency calls at the end of the office-day, after they have seen all the people who came for care and after they have responded to urgent messages. When there are many urgent calls or if the doctor has other after-work commitments, general messages usually wait until the next day. Unfortunately, urgent calls will take precedence on that day too. General calls may wait again.

When you are specific about what you need, the receptionist can route your questions to the staff member assigned to handle that particular issue. This allows them to address your concerns more effectively.

Don't assume the office staff knows how to contact you. Be sure they have current and complete contact information, including daytime, evening, and cell phone numbers. Be specific about the best time and best number to call. A growing number of practices communicate through email or electronic systems like MyChart. Make sure you ask for instructions about how to sign up for the electronic communication system your doctor uses.

Emergencies are in the fabric of medical practice and can disrupt even the most organized schedule. Because of this, the staff may not be able to tell you exactly when the doctor will return your call. Even so, the staff should be able to give you a time frame: morning, afternoon, evening, within twenty-four or forty-eight hours.

## Schedule "Face Time" With the Doctor

Please do not bring several family members to a routine ten- or fifteen-minute office visit and expect an impromptu conference. The doctor will not be able to stop for a prolonged discussion because other people have appointments too. The best way to get the time you need is to *schedule a conference*. Not only is this a better use of time but also when family members hear the information together, there are fewer miscommunications.

If your relative is in a hospital or nursing facility, you may be able to meet the doctor onsite, but you should still try to make the appointment through the doctor's office. In addition to conferences at a facility or in my office, I offered telephone conferences with a speakerphone. As much as possible, my staff tried to schedule the meetings to accommodate local or distant working relatives. Today, the many forms of video conferencing can make this option even more convenient.

## Pick a Point Person

Sometimes conflicting schedules make meetings impossible, even with a conference call. It is unrealistic to expect doctors to schedule individual conferences. Instead, families should pick a point person: someone whom everyone trusts to communicate with the clinical team and relay information to other family members.

## Be Direct but *Nice*

Even if you are frustrated by miscommunication, remember the saying, "You catch more flies with honey." Whether you call, send a letter, or an email to request a conference, be clear about your concerns. Use "I" statements not "You" statements, which people may see as confrontational. For example, "I need..." rather than "You didn't..." Instead of telling people what to do, "You have to...," ask what they can do. "I would appreciate it if you could..." You can get mean later if you need to; it's hard to backtrack if you're mean first.

## Be Prepared to Pay for the Conference

Whether by phone, video, or in person, conferences help families set up the best plan to give excellent care and support caregivers. They also lower healthcare costs by avoiding misunderstandings that cause avoidable visits to emergency rooms and hospitals. Unfortunately, insurance does not usually cover the fees though some long-term care policies will. Medicare and other health insurance programs will do so only if the older adult receives medical attention on the same date, she attends the meeting, and the doctor uses a specific billing code. Seniors who are seriously ill may not be able to participate in the discussion. There are times when a senior's presence can disrupt the care-planning process. This is especially true when senior suffers from dementia, agitation, or mental health conditions and when family discord causes the older adult to react badly to shouting or the negative "vibe" in the room.

I don't understand why families take offense when they have to pay conference fees. I don't understand that. People seem to have no problem paying for conferences with other professionals. *You pay your lawyer, don't you?* In my experience, many families pool resources and pay out-of-pocket for conferences. Ask about fees, accepted methods of payment, and insurance coverage when you make the appointment. Also ask about how available space limits the number of attendees and tell the staff if you need special accommodations.


### If You Are Still Dissatisfied with Communications

Today, medicine is a customer service industry. You deserve respect and excellent care from a trusted health professional. If you believe a doctor is not communicating with you or taking your concerns seriously, it's time to look for a new doctor. My mentor James R. Webster, Jr., MD always said, "Doctors don't have patients; patients have doctors." The core of the patient-doctor relationship is trust. You must do your part to develop effective communication by being specific and open. You must also accept that the most valuable professionals tell you the truth, not what you want to hear. They make recommendations according to current, evidence-based scientific information, the standards of their profession, and their experience. Using these resources, they recommend what they believe is right for your specific situation.

If any health care professional says the problems that concern you are "just old age," get a second opinion. This is the time to look for a geriatrics assessment team.


### Physician Home Visits

Although some physicians make home visits in addition to their work in the office, long-term care facilities, and hospitals, a growing number of companies provide care only in the home. Most home care physicians are Internal Medicine or Family Medicine doctors, and an increasing number are board-certified geriatricians. These professionals can perform geriatrics assessments and provide ongoing primary care for homebound people. This can reduce the unnecessary use of emergency rooms and hospitals.

The American Academy of Home Care Medicine (AAHCM) is active in research and advocacy for better home healthcare policies. They also focus on education for health professionals who want to give state-of-the-art care in the home. The AAHCM website (www.aachm.org) can give you a list of members in your area. Area agencies on aging, state and city departments on aging, medical societies, and physician referral programs are also good sources of information about home care physicians.

Home physician services are becoming more available and they are a valuable resource when appropriate. Unfortunately, when home physicians do not communicate with primary doctors, this can create a parallel care structure that undermines health and safety. It can also lead to medication errors, missed diagnoses, poor health, hospitalization, and higher costs.

If a physician visits you at home and you have a primary care doctor, be sure they work together to coordinate your care. Give the doctors written permission to talk to each other so they can avoid duplicate tests, extra medicine, and conflicting instructions.

If you do not have a primary care doctor, discuss mammograms, colonoscopies, other preventive health screenings, vaccinations, advance directives, and mental health concerns with the home physicians. If they say this isn't their job, find a primary care doctor!

## The Internet is a Place to Get Questions, Not Answers

Many people use Internet search engines to find medical information online. I believe an informed patient is the best partner in care planning, but most do not have training or experience as health care professionals. Even when doctors are patients (or caregivers), the impact of illness, stress, and fear robs them of the most valuable asset any professional offers when serving clients - objectivity. Whether they are health professionals or not, caregivers who expect treatment plans based solely on Internet research do a disservice to people who want to be healthier.

\*\*\*\*\*\*\*\*\*\*\*\*\*\*\*\*\*\*\*\*\*\*\*\*\*

When I was in practice, many people brought advertisements and other information from the Internet, TV and magazines. My recommendations often contradicted these sources. Even so, some people demanded specific tests or treatments based on this information. For example, some people wanted to stop taking their blood pressure or cholesterol medicines because of side-effects listed in the ads.

I informed them that drug companies list rapid-fire cautions and disclaimers to report every side effect that *could* happen in case any of them *do* happen. The companies believe people cannot sue successfully if there is proof that they gave warnings about potential problems. These ads rarely discuss what *usually* happens or how doctors monitor to prevent dangerous side effects. Neither do these ads consider the impact of having more than one illness, and they don't mention situations where the benefits of treatment outweigh the risks.

Sometimes, people believed me, and we negotiated a plan to work together to monitor the condition. Sometimes, they chose to leave my practice.

\*\*\*\*\*\*\*\*\*\*\*\*\*\*\*\*\*\*\*\*\*\*\*\*\*\*

Effective medical decision-making is unique to each person. It requires a thorough review of all the medical facts, symptoms, the effects of other illnesses, allergies, and previous responses to treatment, as well as lifestyle, beliefs, and values.

*A few hours on the Internet does not equal at least seven years of post-college training with a medical degree and license, board certifications, years of experience, and hours of yearly continuing medical education courses.*

Find doctors you trust and put their training and experience to work for you. Identify knowledgeable professionals through recommendations from friends, family, and other people who have chosen the doctor's practice. Investigate training, credentials, and experience. Make sure you agree with the doctor's values, practice style, practice policies, and communication protocols.

An informed patient is the best care partner. Feel free to search for information online and be aware of whether you are reading advertising or medical information. Write down your questions and discuss the information with a healthcare professional you trust. If you don't trust your doctor, find one you can trust and don't let a search engine manage your healthcare.

## Hail HIPAA! The Health Information Portability and Accountability Act

The purpose of the 1996 HIPAA legislation was to:

- Expand and maintain Americans' access to health insurance and retain eligibility despite lapses in coverage due to job changes or unemployment.

- Develop security standards to ensure the privacy of personal health information (PHI).

- Make insurance companies more transparent and less restrictive about how they offer coverage.

- Set up a system to define HIPAA violations and assess penalties.


Thus far, only the privacy and punitive portions of the law are in full force.

Under the privacy provision, HIPAA allows someone to receive another person's health information only with written permission from the person receiving care, or from a designated advocate: a legal guardian, or the person who has Power of Attorney (POA) for healthcare.

Healthcare professionals cannot share PHI with just anyone, no matter how sincere that person may be. We must have written permission from the person or the advocate before we can speak with anyone, even family members.

If the patient cannot give consent, doctors turn to the legal guardian or the POA. If there is no POA, doctors follow the Healthcare Surrogate laws in their state. These determine whom health professionals should consider as next of kin.

When I was in practice, I asked *every adult* to prepare a POA, regardless of age. I also asked everyone to complete and sign a list of the people with whom I could discuss their health issues. The list included instructions about whom I should call first, second, and so on. I asked for this information in the first office visit and reviewed it every year. This strategy proved useful time and again; I had the information before a crisis arose and permission to use it when necessary.

This list of approved contacts also allowed me to diffuse arguments with disgruntled family members. I was able to say, "I'm sorry. He didn't put your name on the list. *I cannot talk to you.* You have to take it up with him."

**Despite HIPAA, You Can Give Useful Information**

HIPAA says a doctor cannot talk to you if you don't have permission from the senior. *HIPAA does **not** say you can't talk to the doctor.* Family members who are not on the list may still have vital information to contribute.

\*\*\*\*\*\*\*\*\*\*\*\*\*\*\*\*\*\*\*\*\*\*\*\*\*\*\*

When a family asked me to investigate Mom's "unexplained falls," I was glad an unlisted family member told me about the beer she drinks every night.

\*\*\*\*\*\*\*\*\*\*\*\*\*\*\*\*\*\*\*\*\*\*\*\*\*\*\*

When I was in practice, I always felt comfortable considering information from an unauthorized person as long as I did not release PHI without permission. When I needed further information, I would try to explore the topic in gentle conversation with the patient or POA.

When family discord or sensitive topics make sending information through the point person difficult, anyone can send a note, e-mail, or a fax to voice concerns. Do not overwhelm the office staff with phone calls or visits, and do not expect a response. HIPAA does not *allow* the doctor to respond. Even so, the information you give can have great impact on your loved one's care.

Though communicating with health professionals is essential in developing solid care plans, nothing will work if you can't communicate with your senior.

# CHAPTER 7

# Work with Your Senior:
## *Communicate for Cooperation*

Geriatrics assessment can be threatening for seniors who fear that the results might take away their independence. Remember who these people are. Today, the oldest seniors include people who suffered with their parents through the Great Depression, survived the Holocaust in Europe, and stormed the beaches at Normandy. Many of their contemporaries created the post-World War II economic boom, shouldered both the Civil Rights and Women's movements, served in Korea, and endured the Vietnam conflict and its fall-out.

The Baby Boomers are the new wave seniors and the first of this generation reached age sixty-five in 2011. Their activism and work ethic caused major social, financial, and political changes as their preferences became policy. None of the current seniors will take kindly to feeling powerless. They are used to tackling obstacles and will not hesitate to fight just because *you* are the current obstacle!

Sometimes, for the senior's sake or for the sake of the community, it is necessary to act despite a senior's refusal. The first step is a geriatrics assessment to determine whether the senior is mentally and physically capable. If they are, they have the right to make decisions. Even if the senior is not capable of sound decision-making, you cannot hold up a legal document and say, "This means you have to get dressed now." Caregiving works better when you can convince the senior to cooperate. Here are some basic rules.

## Pick Your Battles

Don't major in the minor by fighting over things that don't affect health and safety. If a senior wants to sleep on the floor, cover him up. If he wants to shake hot sauce on pancakes, be happy he's eating. Caregivers should honor seniors' wishes unless those wishes are dangerous to them or someone else. Though this may be inconvenient or disruptive to your schedule and sometimes may upset your sensibilities, try to get past it.

You do not have to rearrange every minute of your life, but when you can, as much as you can, let her have her way. It's not giving up; it's giving in to a situation that is not totally under your control. Compromise when safety is not an issue.

## Give as Many Choices as Possible

Does she want to wear the green shirt or the blue one? Does he want toast or a bagel? Does she want to do this or that first? Keep to the schedule of her favorite TV shows, activities, and routines as much as possible. Does he have to have his bath now or can it wait until after *Wheel of Fortune*? Every option you offer should be equally safe, acceptable, and *possible*.

## Don't Give Choices They Cannot Really Have

Don't ask if she wants to go to the adult day center when staying home alone isn't safe, there's no money for hired help, and you cannot take more time off from work. If all else fails, go out to breakfast or a store; end up at the center, and let the staff handle the fallout. The staff can often entice the older adult by recognizing a skill and putting him in a position of "responsibility." Many of my patients saw the center as "going to work." You can also try to sweeten the pot with activities the senior enjoys. "This morning, we will go to the center and tonight we will (enjoy a favorite activity)."

Older adults may feel threatened by a hired caregiver. Even if you have been careful to choose a helper who will show respect and as much affection as the senior will allow, understand that the relationship may take some time to grow. The senior may see this person as a stranger, entering their domain, trying to take over! The senior may be more cooperative if they see this as something that helps *you*. You may be able to soothe seniors' feelings by giving them some power. You might say, "Mrs. Helper is coming today to give me a hand with the housework. Here is a list of other things I thought she should do. Did I miss anything? Do you have any other instructions for her?"

You may have to be there the first few times. You might have to give Mrs. Helper a key. Even so, be sure of yourself. Present the schedule with confidence, do not waver, and *hold your temper.*

### Watch Your Tone of Voice

You may have to make hard decisions and implement them over your seniors' objections however, this is not a role reversal. No matter how disabled they become, no matter how much responsibility you must assume, your parents never become your children; they are always your parents. Your tone of voice should be respectful, never abrupt, and never patronizing. Don't use a voice you would use with a child or say, "Now Mom, you know you can't eat that." This will never work.

Even when my mother no longer recognized me, if I was impatient, spoke too sharply, or spoke to her as if she was a child, she would slap me just as fast as she would have when I was a kid. Even before you stepped in as caregiver, were there times when you thought your parent still saw you as a child? Did you ever wish your mom wouldn't comment so freely on your parenting or other life decisions? I know I did. Once my kids became adults, I came to understand how hard it is to control those reflexes that make parents rush to rescue, protect, and correct. The controls on those reflexes may weaken with illness and with the fear of losing independence. Remember that in some ways, your senior may still see you as a child. How would she have responded if her eight-year-old had challenged her? Can you see why she won't tolerate it now?

Just as in marriage or any other intimate relationship, in eldercare, what you say is often less important than how you say it. Calm, respectful tones are key. Don't argue even when you have to get it done.

### Sometimes You Gotta Do What You Gotta Do

You may have to agree in words, say "yes sir," and then hire people, rearrange the house, and buy things anyway. Unfortunately, this will not work when the senior refuses to bathe, dress, or accept other types of direct personal care. Here, enticements are key.

You will probably never hear your senior say, "You know, hiring this respite worker was really a great idea." If you have had a geriatrics assessment and LOCRx, you know what you need to do. If you have worked with a professional eldercare consultant or other social service advisor, you know how to do it. Don't argue or plead. Be confident. You're right. This is the way it must be. Go on and get it done. Since you have the LOCRx, you can blame it on the doctor. Even so, the senior's verbal response may be deadly.

### Listen with "Big Kid" Ears

In his book, *Marriage on the Rock*, Pastor Jimmy Evans says that though the Bible instructs us to honor our parents, the Book tells only children to obey [17,18,19]. No matter how our parents see us, it's important that we do not hear their comments as if we were still children. I call this skill "hearing with 'Big Kid' ears. This is especially important when our seniors don't want us to do what we must do to keep them safe. It is especially hard for those of us who were the good kids. We stayed out of trouble, were obedient, and enjoyed our parents' approval. Now, we have to disobey because what they want to do is dangerous. He *shouldn't* drive. She *shouldn't* live alone. They *are* messing up their finances. If you do what they tell you to do and leave them in danger, how is that being a good kid?

*************************

I realized my mother shouldn't drive anymore when she drove me and my then eighteen-month-old son to the zoo in Philadelphia (where she had grown up and where she'd always taken my brother and me when we were kids). Road construction caused a minor detour, and Mother became confused. If I had not been with her, she would have gotten lost. The neighbors and my cousins confirmed that Mother often drove too fast or too slowly and moved between lanes without looking. We were blessed that she hadn't yet had an accident.

No amount of reasoning could convince Mother to stop driving. She was insulted and angry and she pushed every one of my "good kid" buttons. Still, one of my cousins and I hatched a plan to make the car disappear and tell her it had been stolen. As a last-ditch effort, we got one of my childhood friends to tell her he needed a car for work. To my great relief, she gave it to him. Although in this case, I was able to continue to be a good kid, I had been totally prepared to lie to my mama. I knew it would be easier to live with lying to her than to get a horrible phone call from the police or an emergency room.

*************************

It's hard to make tough decisions in the face of your senior's objections. It can be uncomfortable, even painful, especially if you've always been a good kid. Just remember, you aren't eight years old; you're forty-eight, fifty-eight, or sixty-eight, right? You're grown and *when you are an adult, respect does not equal obedience.* Also, you don't *need* them to think you're a good kid. You need to investigate your options, get your LOCRx, and feel confident that you're doing the right thing.

When seniors are of sound mind, they have the right to make bad decisions. You have to accept that, but you don't have to be their partner. They won't like it. They know where all your guilt buttons are, and they will push every one of them, so be strong. Hear with big-kid (adult) ears; give honor and respect though not always obedience. Whenever you feel torn between obedience and responsibility, ask yourself this question: *Would I prefer that she's angry with me or that I let something bad happen to her?*

Even when caregivers can navigate difficulties with the senior, many find that their greatest challenges come from interactions with other family members.

# CHAPTER 8

# Get Help from Family and Friends

When we are lucky, caregiving can bring families together around common goals. When we are not lucky, caregiving can open rifts, reveal grudges, and air long-standing conflicts. To help families give more effective care without compromising their relationships, health and joy, I developed:

**The Five Keys to Caregiver Survival.**

    #1  Don't Put Your Head in the Sand: *Find Out If You Need Help*

    #2  Take the "S" Off Your Chest or Step Away from the Kryptonite: *You DO Need Help*

    #3  "Don't Ask, Don't Tell" Won't Work: *Tell People You Need Help*

This key has several important parts.

"Ye Have Not Because Ye Ask Not:" [20]
*You Have to Ask.*

Show Up or Shut Up:
*If They Don't Help, They Can't Criticize.*

Do NOT Accept Responsibility Without Authority:
*If You Give the Care, You Must Have Full Access to the Resources*

"There's no SHOULD; there's only IS." —Eula Morgan Cothran
*Get Help Where You Can, Not Only Where You Expect It.*

#4  If You Don't Want to Drive All the Time, Take Your Hands Off the Steering Wheel: *Let People Help*

#5  Put Your Mask on First: *You Can't Take Care of THEM if You Don't Take Care of YOU.*

The following discussions give explanations and examples for each key. Take your time here (especially with Key #3) If you take nothing else away from this book, I want you to hold on to these five keys.

### #1  Don't Put Your Head in the Sand: *Find Out If You Need Help*

According to folklore, ostriches put their heads in the sand, thinking the danger can't see them if they can't see the danger. We can imagine that these birds are in denial. The problem is that *ostriches get their backsides shot off all the time.* Aren't there ostrich burgers and ostrich steaks in specialty grocery stores? *When you put your head in the sand, you present a bigger target.*

The outcome can be much worse if you pretend that nothing *could* be wrong. In Chapter 3 (*Don't Deny; Don't Delay - D'Nile Ain't Just a River in Egypt*), we saw that Mrs. Miller's son denied her illness and missed opportunities to protect his mother.

We also explored the reasons for caregiver denial in that chapter. Many caregivers believe they are working toward emotional self-preservation when they hide from changes in their relationship with the senior. They are actually trying to avoid another straw on the caregiving camel's back.

It makes sense that people try to deny conditions that will have such drastic impact on everyone's lives. We understand that no one would *choose* to subject herself to that kind of pain. Even so, remember the ostrich. Putting your head in the sand doesn't protect you from the danger; it just allows problems to blindside you.

No matter who raises the question and no matter who takes offense, if *anyone* suggests there might be a problem, get a geriatrics assessment and find out if you need help. If you don't have a problem, everyone will be reassured (or vindicated). If you do, you can start planning. If Mrs. Miller's son (*from Chapter 3*) had done this, he could have avoided physical and financial heartache for his mother and himself.

## #2  Take the "S" Off Your Chest or Step Away from the Kryptonite: *You DO Need Help*

Many caregivers believe they are SUPERCAREGIVER! until a change in their own health, an increase in caregiving responsibilities, or another commitment adds to their burden. Then, they feel like they've encountered Kryptonite that saps the last of their strength.

\*\*\*\*\*\*\*\*\*\*\*\*\*\*\*\*\*\*\*\*\*\*\*\*\*\*

Mr. Sanders described himself as an "independent, tough old coot." He had smoked three packs of cigarettes every day since his teens and struggled with high blood pressure and cholesterol. A series of tiny strokes left Mr. Sander's memory and judgement so poor that he could not manage his finances. He developed emphysema, and shortness of breath caused difficulty with housekeeping and personal care.

His daughter, Carolyn, worked the night shift and had two school-age children. Her husband worked as a consultant in a position that required out-of-town travel at least two weeks every month. Carolyn spent her days helping her father in his home across town and her nights at work; she got very little sleep. Initially, an older neighbor cared for Carolyn's children. As the children grew, they became involved in activities outside of school. The neighbor did not drive, and this made the situation unmanageable.

Although Mr. Sanders argued at first, he agreed to move into his daughter's home. Carolyn thought this would be good for everyone because Mr. Sanders would not have to spend money on housing. She also thought he could help take care of his grandchildren. Unfortunately, Carolyn's son had asthma, and her father did not appreciate having to limit his smoking to the back porch. The move to a less familiar environment also made Mr. Sanders' confusion more obvious, and the active children agitated him.

The next year, Carolyn discovered she was pregnant. Mr. Sanders' memory and function had declined so severely that he needed twenty-four-hour supervision. Carolyn was reluctant to leave her father alone with the children because of his agitation and loud outbursts. At the end of the second trimester of her pregnancy, Carolyn began to have contractions and noted spots of blood in her underwear. Her doctor ordered bed rest for the rest of the pregnancy.

Carolyn and her husband realized this was the last straw. He accepted a management position that required less travel. They moved Mr. Sanders into an assisted-living facility that allowed monitored smoking. Carolyn submitted a request to return to her company in a day position at the end of her maternity leave.

\*\*\*\*\*\*\*\*\*\*\*\*\*\*\*\*\*\*\*\*\*\*\*\*\*\*

It never occurred to Carolyn that it might be too hard to work full-time at night and care for children and a dependent adult during the day without the daily support of her husband. She did not have a realistic view of the number of straws on her camel's back until it broke and made her face the possibility of losing her baby.

Caregivers often fail to realize they have taken on too much. Many caregivers accept full responsibility without question and feel guilty if they buckle under the strain. I ask these caregivers:

*"If someone told you the story you just told me, would you be surprised that they had trouble coping?"*

The universal answer is "no," yet caregivers cannot seem to give themselves the same compassion they would give others in a similar situation. They try to do the impossible and don't accept that it *is* impossible until they have no choice.

### #3 "Don't Ask, Don't Tell" Won't Work: *Tell You Need Help*

Some families keep illness a secret to avoid "airing our dirty laundry" or to protect a loved one's reputation. Either can lead to disaster.

\*\*\*\*\*\*\*\*\*\*\*\*\*\*\*\*\*\*\*\*\*\*\*\*\*\*

The Reverend Dr. Porter was the backbone of his family and for over fifty years was the beloved and respected senior pastor of a large church. Over a three-year period, Pastor Porter's wife noticed increasingly strange behavior. He took off his shirt and asked church members to rub lotion on his back. He repeated the same sermon several times in one month. One day, Pastor Porter went out to visit a parishioner. Twenty minutes later, Mrs. Porter found him sitting in the car in front of the house. He could not remember how to start the car. Pastor burned food, left dish towels on top of the stove, and gave about $10,000 to telemarketers.

Mrs. Porter became reluctant to leave Pastor alone at home. Though she loved creating flower arrangements at a local florist, she considered leaving the job until she remembered that she carried the couple's supplemental health insurance and prescription drug plan.

Reverend and Mrs. Porter had several adult children who lived out of town, a large network of friends, and a huge local church family. Even so, Mrs. Porter did not ask for help. She thought the reverend would be embarrassed if anyone knew he was having trouble.

Mrs. Porter called to check on Pastor several times every day until he stopped answering the telephone. Then, she began to rush home at lunchtime. One day, she sped through a red light and had a car accident that dislocated her shoulder, bruised her knee, and strained her hip.

Mrs. Porter's injury alerted the rest of the family to the problem and showed that she needed other options. The family finally confided their concern to Pastor's primary care physician who referred him to a geriatrician. The diagnosis was dementia. At Mrs. Porter's request, the geriatrics team met with her children and the elders of the church. The team explained Rev. Porter's illness and described his future.

The Porters and their church family decided to give a dinner to honor Pastor's career, celebrate his retirement, and usher him into the role of Pastor Emeritus. Several retired friends and deacons rotated the responsibility of visiting Pastor, taking him to lunch, and accompanying him on visits to see the sick and shut-in. Rev. Porter enjoyed the attention and never recognized it as the supervision it was. As Reverend Porter's condition declined, Mrs. Porter and their children began to investigate ways to finance adult day services and other care resources they might need in the future.

\*\*\*\*\*\*\*\*\*\*\*\*\*\*\*\*\*\*\*\*\*\*\*\*

Don't hide disability from other family members, neighbors, church members, or business associates. Disability is not a character flaw. Also, you need all the help you can get. It takes a village to support a senior as it does to raise a child; everyone's eyes, ears, hands, and ideas will be useful.

\*\*\*\*\*\*\*\*\*\*\*\*\*\*\*\*\*\*\*\*\*\*\*\*

We were able to keep my mother in her home much longer because of Mr.

Scott. He had lived across the alley for fifty years and knew when Mother's lights were supposed to go off at night. If they did not go off when he expected, he called her. If she didn't answer or what she said didn't make sense, Mr. Scott called a family member.

\*\*\*\*\*\*\*\*\*\*\*\*\*\*\*\*\*\*\*\*\*\*\*\*\*

Tell people you need help, but this key to caregiver survival has several important caveats:

### *"Ye Have Not Because Ye Ask Not:"* [20]
### *You Have to Ask*

Some caregivers believe they should not have to ask for help, yet they feel bitter when relatives don't step up with spontaneous offers. It isn't fair for caregivers to expect people to read their minds.

\*\*\*\*\*\*\*\*\*\*\*\*\*\*\*\*\*\*\*\*\*\*\*\*\*

Mr. and Mrs. Billings had been married for sixty years when she had a stroke. Mr. Billings tried to take his wife everywhere with him, but she could not walk well, and she tired easily. Then, he became a full-time caregiver. He also took care of the house, yard, car, finances, laundry, and cooking. After several months, he was so worn out that he stopped playing cards, missed bowling with his friends, and became isolated.

Mr. and Mrs. Billings both had siblings who visited regularly though Mr. Billings was angry that none of them offered to "help more." He never asked for help directly, and his sisters thought he seemed to have everything under control. Finally, Mr. Billings admitted he needed more time to himself. He asked one of his sisters to spend a few hours a week with Mrs. Billings so he could spend time with his friends. His sister was happy to help.

\*\*\*\*\*\*\*\*\*\*\*\*\*\*\*\*\*\*\*\*\*\*\*\*\*

Don't assume that people know what you need. Don't expect them to read your mind or recognize needs that are obvious to you. They might be willing to help if you let them know you need it.

**Be specific**. "Why don't you give me more help with Mom?" is too vague. Once a geriatrician prescribes the LOCRx, you should say, "The doctor says Dad needs A, B, and C. I've done A. Can you do B or C by next

Thursday (or another specific time)?

This language is precise and diplomatic. First, it makes it clear that you did not decide what the needs are. The directions come from the professional level of care prescription (LOCRx). This strategy also shows that you have done A; you accepted a role and are not dumping on the other family members. It gives them a choice of tasks: B or C. Again, they don't feel like you are telling them what to do. Finally, this strategy outlines a specific time frame, which lets you know exactly how long to wait before you move to your back-up plan and find other helpers.

### Show Up or Shut Up:
### If They Don't Help, They Can't Criticize

Influential and assertive family members may have strong opinions about the care plan and often voice their disapproval in no uncertain terms. Caregivers may act on these opinions even though the recommendations are unrealistic, come without offers of help, or with promised help that does not appear.

\*\*\*\*\*\*\*\*\*\*\*\*\*\*\*\*\*\*\*\*\*\*\*\*\*\*

Mrs. King was a tireless community advocate until she developed heart failure. Arthritis in her spine pinched nerves in her back. This caused pain and muscle weakness in her legs, but her heart was too weak for an operation. Mrs. King suffered several falls and had a minor car accident when she couldn't move her foot from the gas pedal to the brake fast enough for a safe stop. Over time, Mrs. King became so short of breath that she it was hard for her to walk or take care of herself. She also had several small strokes and developed memory loss that made her forget to pay bills. Then, she got lost driving to the senior center where she ate lunch every day. It was clear that she could no longer live alone in her third-floor, walk-up apartment.

Mrs. King had three children, though only her youngest daughter, Natalie, visited regularly. She took her mother to the doctor and assisted with her medicines, laundry, housekeeping, and grocery shopping. Natalie also worked full-time and was a night-student in a master's degree program.

Mrs. King had several sisters in the same community. They had visited their sister rarely and only at their convenience. They did not invite her to their homes, nor include her in their outings. Despite this, they were very vocal in their opinions about Mrs. King's care. Even though Natalie asked, they offered neither help nor financial support.

As her mother's health deteriorated, Natalie considered an assisted-living community or moving Mrs. King to a first-floor apartment with hired help in the home. Mrs. King's sisters insisted that Natalie owed it to their sister to stop working, move in with her mother, and use her own funds to pay for a chair lift. Natalie respected her aunts and did not want to argue with them. Although she did not move into her mother's apartment, she juggled her schedule and finances to care for her mother alone. Within a year, Natalie was worn out and financially stressed.

After becoming involved in a caregiver support group, Natalie found strength to withstand her aunts' assaults and make a workable plan. She moved her mother to a first-floor apartment, used Mrs. King's money to hire a caregiver, and arranged daily transportation to the senior center. Her aunts kept complaining, and Natalie kept taking care of her mother and herself.

\*\*\*\*\*\*\*\*\*\*\*\*\*\*\*\*\*\*\*\*\*\*\*\*\*\*

Sometimes, family members offer no help, or they agree to help, fail to follow through, and still feel entitled to comment on the care plan. They don't get to do that!

## COMMITMENT + ACCOUNTABILITY = ENTITLEMENT

No matter how old they are or how much power they have in the family, relatives must commit to doing something and *do* it before they have the right to complain. If they fail to keep those commitments, it is unfair for them to criticize. (See *Chapter 5: Really! Don't Despair - The Family Conference*).

You do not have to tell anyone to show up or shut up. You want to have Thanksgiving dinner next year, right? Instead, let your behavior speak for itself. Tell family members about the LOCRx you got from the doctor. Use the "A, B, C" language I recommended in the *Be Specific* portion of this chapter to ask relatives which tasks they can manage. Then, hold them accountable for the help they offer.

If they don't keep their word, go on and do what you need to do. When they complain about your decision, you can say, "The doctor said Mom needs A, B, and C. I said I could do A and I did it. Didn't you agree to do B or C? If B and C had happened, I wouldn't have had to (whatever you chose to do because you didn't have help)." Be prepared to repeat this mantra *every time* someone wants to talk without putting any skin in the game.

In my experience, when caregivers take this position, mouthy family members either step up to help, or they step aside. One caregiver said she found another useful response: "I understand you feel that way. If you want to do something different, go ahead." Mouthy family members sputtered, did nothing, and stopped pestering her.

Whether you choose to respond or ignore, I find that it's best not to argue. Arguments rarely change the non-helper's behavior. They just increase your stress.

While it makes sense that you would feel guilty when you ignore family members' comments, try to do it anyway. They earned it. Understand that these people gave up the right to comment on caregiving decisions when they refused to help. Go on and get the job done in a way that works best for your senior and yourself.

*Do NOT Accept Responsibility Without Authority:*
*If You Give the Care, You Must Have Full Access to the Resources*

Many caregivers are on the front line while someone else controls the purse strings, and that person just doesn't get it.

\*\*\*\*\*\*\*\*\*\*\*\*\*\*\*\*\*\*\*\*\*\*\*\*\*\*\*

After years of hard drinking, Mr. Owens developed heart failure and liver disease. His legs were swollen; he walked slowly and often forgot to take his medicine. He lived in his home with his daughter, Eliza, who worked nights in a bakery. His son, Andrew, was a successful lawyer who lived downtown. Because of his son's profession and status as the eldest child, Mr. Owens had chosen Andrew as POA for healthcare and finance, executor of his will, and co-signer on all financial accounts. There were no other family members.

Eliza got home at 6 a.m. every morning; she cooked breakfast for her dad, gave him his medicine, prepared the other meals, cleaned the house, and did laundry before going to bed at about 2 p.m. She left for work around 10:30 p.m., after bathing her dad and putting him to bed.

Mr. Owens woke his daughter several times during the afternoon and evening. He also called her frequently through the night, complaining that someone was in the house. Sleep interruptions left Eliza exhausted, and the phone calls caused problems with her employer.

FedEx delivered packages to the house every day. Although Mr. Owens denied ordering anything, the packages were filled with merchandise from his favorite television shopping shows. He also hid the packages, and Eliza often found them too late to return them for refunds. Even if she found them within the return period, shipping was costly. She worried about finances; she worried about leaving her dad alone, and she worried about keeping her job.

Eliza needed to curb Mr. Owens's spending, get some rest, work without interruptions, and find time to relax with friends. She asked her brother to help by calling their dad in the evenings and taking him out for a few hours on the weekends. Andrew agreed wholeheartedly, yet every time Eliza asked for a specific time, he gave her a list of his many commitments. Andrew saw no reason to cancel Mr. Owens's credit cards, use their dad's money to hire help, or arrange adult day services. Every time Eliza tried to convince her brother that their father needed help, Andrew made light of her concerns. He said, "Dad has always worked hard. Why shouldn't he buy whatever he wants?"

One of the neighbors agreed to help Eliza by sitting with her father for a few hours three evenings a week and every other weekend. One winter night, when the neighbor was not scheduled to be with Mr. Owens, she called Eliza at work to say that he had come to her home at midnight wearing pajamas without shoes or a coat. Since she was unable to convince Mr. Owens to come into her house, the neighbor walked him home and called his daughter. Eliza left work early. The bakery manager was not pleased.

Andrew wasn't concerned about their father's midnight trek in the snow either. "Dad just needed to stretch his legs," he said and accused his sister of being too eager to restrict their father's independence. Andrew also said Eliza was selfish and ungrateful. "You left Dad with a stranger after all he's done for us!"

Eliza felt angry and heartbroken. She had always looked up to her big brother and did not want to fight with him. Though she wanted to take care of their dad, she knew she could not continue under the current conditions. She gave her brother several options.

- Take more responsibility for their dad's direct care.
- Respect her concerns about their dad's needs and give full emotional and financial support.
- Give up his power of attorney and agree not to contest his sister's petition for guardianship of Mr. Owens.

Eliza also said she would move out and leave her brother with both *responsibility and authority* if he did not get with the program. Her ultimatum shocked Andrew into action. He agreed to a comprehensive geriatrics assessment for Mr. Owens and worked with his sister to put the LOCRx into action. They protected their dad's money and his dignity by leaving him one, low-limit credit card. They used his funds to hire workers for evenings and weekends and arranged respite care so Eliza could take vacations.

\*\*\*\*\*\*\*\*\*\*\*\*\*\*\*\*\*\*\*\*\*\*\*\*\*\*

Eliza was Mr. Owens' primary caregiver while her brother had the right to make all the financial and healthcare decisions. Not only was this unfair, it was also ineffective in providing the safety Mr. Owens needed. If you have direct caregiving responsibility, you cannot let anyone tie your hands. Frontline caregivers must have a major role in deciding how to use financial resources for care. If the caregiver is not the guardian or POA, the person with that authority must be a full partner. If you have responsibility without authority, believe me, the people with authority will rethink the situation if you offer to step out and let them have both.

*"There's no SHOULD; there's only IS."*
*Get Help Where You Can Not Only Where You Expect it*
—Eula Morgan Cothran

My grandmother used to say this whenever we complained that things *shouldn't* be the way they are. Some caregivers refuse help from willing people because they think only *certain* family members *should* help.

\*\*\*\*\*\*\*\*\*\*\*\*\*\*\*\*\*\*\*\*\*\*\*\*\*

Ms. Lee was a computer science professional for a local school system. She was also a single mother with a school-age son and preschool twins. Ms. Lee's mother had Parkinson's disease with mobility challenges that made it hard for her to shop for groceries and clean her house.

Ms. Lee had a wide circle of friends, church members, and co-workers, and she had always been quick to help anyone in need. Whenever anyone asked how she was, though Ms. Lee always said, "Blessed and highly favored," everyone could see that she looked haggard.

Friends offered to pick up extra items for Mrs. Lee's mother when they went grocery shopping. A church sister offered to send a member of the youth group over to the senior's house to do laundry and light cleaning once a week. She also offered to sign Ms. Lee's mother up for the youth group's program to cut grass and shovel snow for seniors in need. A co-worker offered to make extra food when she cooked and bring it to work to give Ms. Lee's mom an easy meal or two.

Ms. Lee thanked everyone but declined all help saying, "Mom has five children." Ms. Lee did not think her mother "should have to rely on strangers." One sister helped manage Mom's finances, but she was a nurse and pulled twelve-hour night shifts in the hospital. She also spent several hours each week as a room-mom for her son's kindergarten class. Another sister and two brothers were not involved.

Ms. Lee continued to visit her mother after work almost every day, doing laundry, cleaning, cooking, or shopping for groceries. She declined help when a neighbor offered to cut the grass and kept calling her brother to do it even though he never answered.

One evening, Ms. Lee rushed to pick up her children from daycare and arrived late again. The administrator met her at the door with a bill for $200 in late fees and demanded payment before the children could return. She also gave notice that the next time Ms. Lee picked her children up late, she would have to dis-enroll them.

\*\*\*\*\*\*\*\*\*\*\*\*\*\*\*\*\*\*\*\*\*\*\*\*\*

Ms. Lee needed to stop worrying about whom she thinks *should* help, and so should you. Get help where you can. As I said before, it takes a village to care for a senior just as it does to raise a child. Who said only blood relatives can be part of the village?

### Yes, Tell the Senior's Employer. Don't Risk Their Benefits

Kirk Riddle is one of the caregivers in my practice, and he made me aware of this important issue. His wife, Lois, was a high-level educational administrator who had early-onset Alzheimer's disease. Kirk teaches that it is important to inform employers so they address the condition as a medical problem before it becomes a job-performance issue. If you conceal a disabling condition, you risk termination and the loss of employer-based benefits.

\*\*\*\*\*\*\*\*\*\*\*\*\*\*\*\*\*\*\*\*\*\*\*\*\*

Mrs. deBrill was a widow, and her adult children lived out of state. She had been a respected math teacher for almost forty years before she began to have trouble using the keyboard on her computer. This made it hard to post grades on time. Mrs. deBrill started to drop coffee mugs and stumble. Getting dressed in the morning became a struggle, and she was late for work several times every week.

Mrs. deBrill's doctor diagnosed inflammation in her muscles and nerves caused by an abnormal reaction of her immune system. She stopped taking medicine that might slow progression of the illness because she did not want her students and co-workers to notice the swelling it caused in her face, hands, and legs.

The principal was embarrassed when she had to inform Mrs. deBrill that unless things improved, there would be disciplinary action. Mrs. deBrill continued to have problems with her health and performance. Eventually, she retired to avoid termination. Since she did not complete forty years of employment, she could not take advantage of the special bonus she had been counting on to help her move into a life care community with exercise facilities, transportation, an exciting travel and activity program, and all levels of care from independent-living through hospice.

\*\*\*\*\*\*\*\*\*\*\*\*\*\*\*\*\*\*\*\*\*\*\*\*\*\*

Once you have the LOCRx, you will know the severity and prognosis of the condition, as well as what your loved one can and cannot do. Discuss this with the employer. It might be possible to arrange job-site accommodations.

If you wait for termination, continued income, non-vested pension funds, and other benefits will be at risk. These include Family Medical Leave (FMLA), which provides unpaid leave with job security. There is also short- or long-term medical or disability leave, which provides partial salary without guarantee of future employment. With termination, neither types of leave will be available.

Hiding a disability to protect a person's reputation can risk more than finances. Memory loss or physical conditions that change the ability to drive, operate machinery, or maintain safety protocols can endanger the senior, other workers, caregivers, and the whole community. Work with employers to obtain the maximum human resource benefits, and allow the senior to exit high-profile responsibilities with dignity and respect.

### #4 If You Don't Want to Drive All the Time, Take Your Hands Off the Steering Wheel: *Let People Help*

Some people make caregiving more difficult by discouraging potential helpers.

\*\*\*\*\*\*\*\*\*\*\*\*\*\*\*\*\*\*\*\*\*\*\*\*\*\*

Recall Mr. Billings whose sister agreed to stay with his wife while he had fun with friends. One Saturday afternoon, his sister relieved him. When Mr. Billings returned, he was irritated because Sister had made turkey instead of tuna sandwiches for lunch. Instead of watching television, they had folded laundry. Mr. Billings was sure his wife had been upset by the changes and explained, "She doesn't want anyone doing for her but me. I know how she likes things. I know she called for me the whole time." After this, Sister came for short visits but no longer offered to help.

\*\*\*\*\*\*\*\*\*\*\*\*\*\*\*\*\*\*\*\*\*\*\*\*\*\*

If you want people to help you, let them do it without hovering or being critical. Of course, if the doctor prescribes specific food, medicines, or treatments, you must insist that helpers follow the directions. Also, tell people about the senior's preferences, favorite activities, or comforting schedules that make caregiving easier. Other than giving these helpful hints, don't major in the minor (worry about things that really don't matter). For example, why do you care if Mom wears the blue shirt or the green one? Why fight about or even mention that? As long as the clothing is comfortable and clean, why bother?

\*\*\*\*\*\*\*\*\*\*\*\*\*\*\*\*\*\*\*\*\*\*\*\*\*\*

My mother loved Brook Benton, Count Basie, and Motown. I told the nursing home staff to play one of Mother's favorite tunes and let her dance if she became agitated. The nurses appreciated information that made their work easier. I insisted that Mother wear her own eye glasses and dentures. Otherwise, as long as the shoes and clothes were comfortable and clean, I didn't care what she wore. The nurses were relieved about that too.

\*\*\*\*\*\*\*\*\*\*\*\*\*\*\*\*\*\*\*\*\*\*\*\*\*\*

Caregivers often insist "no one can do it as well as I can." Mr. Billings assumed his wife had called for him all afternoon, but how did he know? He wasn't there. Some caregivers insist on giving care alone because they get their sense of worth from caregiving. (See *Chapter 11: Protect Your Emotional Health - Are You Codependent?*) Others want to make amends for past problems in the relationship. Regardless of the reason, many caregivers make sure that no one else has a chance to help.

Some caregivers believe they can prevent further disability or even death by controlling every aspect of care. They are in great danger. Despite their best efforts, these caregivers cannot change the past nor prevent the inevitable worsening of chronic diseases. When the people they care for die, if these caregivers feel they have failed, they may sink into serious depression.

People will not want to be part of your support team if you micromanage. Let people help you. If you can't do that, work with a counselor to find out why.

### #5 Put Your Mask on First: *You Can't Take Care of THEM if You Don't Take Care of YOU.*

Flight attendants instruct airline passengers to do this in an emergency. Many air travelers read, fall asleep, or otherwise ignore the safety demonstration. Caregivers can't afford to ignore these instructions.

\*\*\*\*\*\*\*\*\*\*\*\*\*\*\*\*\*\*\*\*\*\*\*\*\*\*\*

When I was in practice, a fifty-seven-year-old caregiver died of a heart attack and left two eighty-year-old people alone. She knew exactly when their prescriptions would run out but didn't realize that she hadn't seen her doctor in more than two years. Her blood pressure was out of control, and she didn't know she had developed diabetes. This caregiver had a heart attack because she was too busy taking care of seniors to take care of herself. She could have avoided this and so can you. Here's one caregiver who did.

\*\*\*\*\*\*\*\*\*\*\*\*\*\*\*\*\*\*\*\*\*\*\*\*\*\*\*

Mrs. Green worked, took care of her home and family, and supported her grandfather (whom she called "Pop"). He lived in a community nearby. It was hard to cook, clean, and do laundry at two places. Even bringing Pop's laundry to her home and taking a weeks-worth of meals to fill his freezer became too much for Mrs. Green as her children and their activities grew. The travelling made her late to work so often that she got a written warning from her boss. That's when Pop moved in with the Greens.

Pop was unhappy with the move because he was alone in a strange neighborhood all day and many evenings. The situation wasn't working for Mrs. Green either. Despite adjusting her work and activity schedule, she often got to the pharmacy too late to pick up Pop's medicine and hers. She missed his dentist appointment and forgot her mammogram. Her blood pressure was not well controlled, and she was exhausted. Strained relationships with her husband, kids, and social networks left her feeling stressed and isolated.

Pop grumbled, but Mrs. Green coaxed him to try a senior community near her where he has meals, laundry services, and housekeeping. Now, he plays pool and cards and goes on trips. Mrs. Green calls every day; other family members stop by a couple times a week (when they can find him), and he comes over for dinner on Sundays and holidays. Mrs. Green and her husband schedule date-nights, and she has occasional spa time with girlfriends. She juggles everything with her kids' activities. Her blood pressure is normal, and she has had all her preventive health screenings.

Mrs. Green is working on life-balance. It doesn't always work easily, but she is aware that her health, her needs, and other relationships are important. She is trying to make them a priority.

✳✳✳✳✳✳✳✳✳✳✳✳✳✳✳✳✳✳✳✳✳✳✳✳✳

You can't help anyone if you are demoralized, exhausted, or sick. Don't wait until you're about to drop. Get help early in the caregiving process. Schedule regular breaks so you can look forward to time for yourself. After routine, consistent rest periods, you come back a stronger and better caregiver.

In the Section One of this book, The Crisis in Caregiving, you learned why caregiving is so much harder for you than it was for past generations. In Section Two, you learned how to manage the Challenge of Caregiving by being sure what your senior needs (LOCRx) and by working effectively with professionals and family members who can support you in giving the best care. You also learned the Five Keys to Caregiver Survival, which empower you to use your support team and remind you to also take care of yourself. In Section Three, you'll learn about The Costs of Caregiving and the consequences of *not* taking care of yourself. I want you to understand why you *should* take care of yourself, and I'll give you specific tips on how to do it.

# The Costs of Caregiving: *Protect Your Senior's Most Valuable Resource...You!*

Studies show that many caregivers feel great satisfaction from helping someone in need. Some believe that learning to handle the tough tasks builds character, skills, and confidence. Others believe the experience strengthens relationships with the people who receive care. These caregivers appreciate the opportunity to show gratitude to someone who cared for, guided, and helped to shape them[21].

Whether caregivers feel satisfaction, personal growth, or gratitude, many are so invested in caregiving that they forget they are important, too. We aren't used to thinking of ourselves. We think it's selfish when it's actually, self-care.

**Selfish** is, "I don't care about anybody but myself."

**Self-care** is, "I care about myself too."

Caregivers who can't tell the difference cause hardship for themselves and everyone else.

In the next chapters, you'll meet caregivers who succumb to illness, endanger their marriages and other relationships, neglect their children, strain their finances, and descend into mental health crises while caregiving. This happened because they didn't accept that their needs are also important. The effect is not only devastating for the caregivers but when they are too damaged to give good care, it also hurts the people they thought they were protecting.

# CHAPTER 9

# Protect Your Physical Health:
## *Avoid Your Loved One's Fate*

Many caregivers tell me they are afraid of looking like the people they care for. Past studies have shown that caregivers suffer more stress, depression, chronic illness, and early death than people of the same age who are not giving care. This is especially true for caregivers of people with dementia.[22]

The health and wellness information available on the Internet is more extensive than I can review in this book. Caregivers should discuss this information with their doctors and plan to avoid the health challenges their parents face. Visit my website, www.drcherylwoodson.com, to get your copy of my free the worksheet, *You Should Know These Numbers Like You Know Your Social Security Number.* The worksheet lists health screening tests and other wellness practices to discuss with your doctor every year.

Neither worksheets, books, the Internet, nor other sources of health information are substitutes for your doctor's advice. The most important step in protecting your health is to find a primary care professional to partner with you in developing a specific healthcare plan.

### *You Micromanage Their Health While Ignoring Your Own*

Several years ago, I participated in a National Public Radio program with a PhD immunobiologist. The radio host asked us why caregivers have poorer health than other adults of the same age. The scientist insisted that stress-related damage to the immune system is the primary problem. I majored in Biology in college; I love the subject and don't doubt that immunology plays a big role. However, we don't need biology to explain most caregivers' health problems. The major culprit is self-neglect.

You call for Mom's prescription refills long before she runs out of medicine. Her appointments are etched in your brain, and you follow all the doctors' instructions to control her blood pressure. How often do you forget to fill your prescriptions? When is the last time you saw *your* doctor? Do you know what your blood pressure is?

Researchers reported that over half the caregivers they surveyed skip their own doctor appointments. [23] Missed appointments usually mean missed health screenings. For example, though doctors recommend yearly mammograms for women over age fifty, I know several caregivers who haven't had a mammogram in five years. It is impossible to give good care if you neglect yourself. Who will care for your loved ones if something happens to you?

\*\*\*\*\*\*\*\*\*\*\*\*\*\*\*\*\*\*\*\*\*\*\*\*\*\*

Mr. Jones is a sixty-seven-year-old man who cares for his eighty-seven-year-old mother. Her mind is clear, but she has heart failure and is confined to a chair. She needs help with personal care, getting in and out of bed, and going to the bathroom. Mr. Jones's only family is a brother and sister-in-law who live in another state. They call often and visit when they can.

Before retirement, Mr. Jones was active in his local Masonic lodge. He played handball with his friends and was one of the best bowlers on his team. He also joined them at baseball and basketball games, movies, and other social gatherings. Now, Mr. Jones leaves his mom only long enough to buy groceries and gas.

He retired three years early to care for his mother and makes ends meet on a retirement income that is smaller than he planned. Since he stopped working, Mr. Jones has gained about forty pounds; his knees hurt and he has less energy. Because of pain, fatigue, and caregiving responsibilities, he no longer bowls or plays handball, and he turns down social invitations. After years of trying, his friends don't call as often.

Mr. Jones used to work in a smoke-free environment and smoked only on breaks. He was so busy with his social life that he rarely smoked in the evenings or on weekends. Since he retired, he has chain-smoked a pack and a half of cigarettes every day.

Every night, after he puts his mom to bed, Mr. Jones does laundry, cleans the house, pays bills, and cooks for the next day. He sleeps poorly and fills his night hours watching videos, drinking at least a six-pack of beer, and trying to convince himself he isn't lonely.

Mr. Jones's last physical examination was just before he retired. His doctor warned him that his cholesterol was high and that he was at risk for diabetes. Mr. Jones continued to take the medicine until his refills ran out. Although he took excellent care of his mother and her health, he never made time to go back to the doctor for treatment, preventive care, or prescription refills.

One evening, Mr. Jones was too tired to take out the garbage before trash day as he usually did. The next morning, he waved to a couple of neighbors as he hurried to drag the cans to the curb before the truck came. One neighbor commented that Mr. Jones seemed out of breath, and he admitted that he had felt "short-winded and a little nauseous off and on, especially carrying groceries up the steps." Mr. Jones laughed when the neighbor said, "Maybe you should get a checkup," but as he set the last can by the curb, he began rub his left arm. He also started to sweat and seemed to have more trouble breathing before he collapsed on the sidewalk. The neighbors called an ambulance, and the emergency room doctors pronounced Mr. Jones dead from a heart attack. His mother went into a nursing home.

✶✶✶✶✶✶✶✶✶✶✶✶✶✶✶✶✶✶✶✶✶✶✶✶

Mr. Jones gave care alone. Instead of putting a team in place to support him in caring for his mother, he became isolated and unhealthy. With help, he could have maintained his income and his retirement plan, continued to enjoy his social activities, avoided depression, and created joy. He could also have worked with a primary care physician to manage his arthritis pain, control his alcohol intake, stop smoking, achieve a healthy weight, and reduce his risk of heart disease. Instead, he behaved as if he did not deserve to be happy and healthy. Why would he do that? Why would you?

Even if Mr. Jones had not died, he could have ended up in a nursing home along with his mother. Who would have been *his* advocate or caregiver?

If you can't take care of yourself for your own sake, consider the goals you have for your senior. After Mr. Jones's death, his mother had to live in a facility without an advocate. If his goal was to give her personalized care in her own home, how did neglecting himself achieve that? It did not. Mr. Jones failed himself and his mom because he did not understand that his needs were important too. Let's look at how caregivers can avoid Mr. Jones's situation.

In Chapter 1, we saw that Americans are living *longer*. The key to living *better* is protecting our health in the earlier adult years. Most American caregivers are between forty and seventy years old; *at forty, you're planning for age eighty*. The question is, "Will you *want* to be alive when you reach your eighties and beyond?" If you are healthy, active, and happy, why not? Invest in your health now and give yourself a better chance of living the way you want to live in your golden years.


### *Apply Eldercare Principles to Your Own Care: Don't Deny, Don't Delay, Don't Despair, and Don't Forget to Organize.*

**Don't Deny.** Many people avoid doctors and screening tests because they are afraid to discover that something is wrong. In Chapter 8 (*Get Help from Family and Friends, section - The Five Keys to Caregiver Survival*), we talked about what happens to ostriches. When you put your head in the sand, you present a bigger target. Whether you address a problem or not, the problem is still there, and it *will* affect you.

**Don't Delay.** Try to handle potential health problems before they handle you and destroy your health. Though you might fear the results, don't leave pain, bleeding, weight loss, or other uncomfortable symptoms unchecked. By the time the symptoms are severe enough to demand your attention, a result that was only possible could be all too real. A problem that might have responded to minor treatment could be much worse.

Advances in medical science have allowed doctors to find many illnesses early enough to prevent illness, delay complications, or even cure the condition. Still, some of us will get bad news. The earlier we know, the quicker we can act to improve or control the problem. Early detection also allows more time to make plans to decrease the impact of the condition on our families.

**Don't Despair and Organize Your Health Information.** See your doctor regularly to get the information and treatments you need to stay as healthy as possible. Remember *Chapter 4: Don't Despair- There IS Help, Bernie Ryan's Binder*. Bring the binder to all your doctor visits along with your "brown bag" of prescription and over-the-counter medicines. Visit my website, www.drcherylwoodson.com, to get your copy of the form I recommend to manage your medicines. Don't forget to record all your appointments on the same calendar as your senior's. Update the calendar frequently, and consult it when you schedule an office visit, test, or activities for your senior, other family members, or yourself. This will avoid scheduling conflicts that can tempt you to cancel your appointments.

Remember the fifth of the Five Keys to Caregiver Survival, Put Your Mask on First (See *Chapter 8*). On airplanes, flight attendants tell you to put on *your* mask before you offer to help someone else. You can't take care of THEM if you don't take care of YOU. Physical health is one priority. There are others.

# CHAPTER 10

# Protect Your Financial Health: *The DOs and DON'Ts*

Some caregivers destroy their current finances and compromise their retirement security. Others maintain their financial stability by depending on the seniors in their care. Both situations are dangerous. To avoid them, make sure you understand the DOs and DON'Ts of protecting your financial health.

### DO Protect Your Current Financial Stability

If mid-life adults intend to avoid dooming themselves to poverty in their senior years, they must find ways to stay in the workforce and protect their income, pensions, and insurance benefits.

*Protect Your Income.*

\*\*\*\*\*\*\*\*\*\*\*\*\*\*\*\*\*\*\*\*\*\*\*\*\*\*

Ms. MacNeil had traveled the world as a freelance photographer. Eight years ago, she saw her dad aging and decided to take a less lucrative, full-time position with a local media service. Her father became ill and she planned to take a short leave of absence to care for him until doctors informed her that his condition would cause chronic disability.

Although Mr. MacNeil would no longer be able to live alone, he did not have memory problems, nor did he need skilled nursing care. He did need supportive care for meals, housekeeping, and supervision. The doctor and social worker recommended an income-adjusted, assisted-living facility with meals, housekeeping, and social activities. However, Ms. MacNeil insisted, "Daddy shouldn't have to give up his home." She gave up her apartment and moved in with him.

Although the state assessed that Mr. MacNeil's physical condition required only eight hours of homemaker services per week, neither he nor his daughter felt comfortable that he was alone for most of the day and evening. Instead of paying rent, Ms. MacNeil hired caregivers to cover gaps that occurred during her working hours. She also stayed with her dad every night and on weekends. Her work attendance suffered when caregivers came late or needed to leave early. Ms. MacNeil took time from her work responsibilities to call home several times a day. She also returned to work late after rushing home at lunchtime several times a week. Within months, Ms. MacNeil was exhausted and had used up her savings, sick leave, and vacation time. She had also received written warnings about tardiness and job performance.

Ms. MacNeil was a divorcee without children or siblings. She saw no alternative other than to quit her job to care for her dad full-time. She had not paid into Social Security nor set up an individual retirement account (IRA) when she was self-employed. Neither had she worked in her new position long enough to have significant pension funds. At age fifty-seven, she was eight years away from being eligible for Medicare and at that time, the Affordable Care Act (ACA) had not yet been passed. Financial insecurity left Ms. MacNeil in constant fear of costly disasters: house and car repairs and any accident or illness that might need an emergency room visit.

\*\*\*\*\*\*\*\*\*\*\*\*\*\*\*\*\*\*\*\*\*\*\*\*\*\*

Caregivers often deplete financial resources that would have brought them comfort in their senior years. Many come to work late, leave early, or miss work all together. Others reduce their work hours or make other changes that decrease their incomes. Still more caregivers suffer from what human resource experts and caregiving researchers call "presenteeism:" their bodies are at work while their minds are with their beloved seniors.

I did not find any data on the number of caregiving employees who fail to earn promotions and bonuses because of disciplinary actions nor those who decline positions with higher responsibility (and salaries) to reserve hours for caregiving. Without these data, there is no way to calculate the full impact of caregiving on the finances of working adults. We do know that many working caregivers retire early without adequate retirement savings and until the Affordable Care Act, without health insurance.

It made sense that Ms. MacNeil and her father wanted to keep him in his home. Unfortunately, at each step, Ms. MacNeil did not consider all options. Neither did she think about the long-term financial impact of her decisions. Maybe she couldn't. Maybe her heart wouldn't let her consider alternatives. However, if the MacNeils had been able to make the decision to use an assisted-living situation, Ms. MacNeil would have been able to keep working. She could have enjoyed continued income, health insurance, and paid time off for vacations and her health needs. She could have had several more years to strengthen her retirement plan. Instead of paying for caregivers, Ms. MacNeil could have maintained her savings as a financial cushion. She might also have had less stress, more time to enjoy herself, and a chance to spend *good* time with her dad. Instead, she gave him an anxious, isolated, bedraggled caregiver without income, savings, or investments: a caregiver who had ensured her own poverty in aging.

I know it hurts to decide against giving direct care yourself. Still, it is unwise to quit your job, reduce your work hours, and allow your income to drop until it can't support you now or in retirement. If you choose to retire early, be sure you are vested in your pension or have enough savings, income, or assets to secure your senior years.

*Manage Your Debt*

Many of us find too much month left at the end of the money, and it's not always because of low incomes. Even high-earners can find themselves in financial sinkholes that drain cash reserves and wreck credit. Some reasons are: overspending, high-interest on credit card balances, huge mortgages with declining property values, and predatory "pay-day" and car title loans. Most of us know of communities where people are upside-down in mortgages on mansions and struggle to keep the lights on, even though a BMW sits in the driveway. People who live check to check are slaves no matter how large those checks are.

Many of us have no financial reserves. In December 2018 through January 2019, the federal government shut down for about a month. People lost two paychecks, and there were news reports about missed mortgage and credit card payments. In 2020, COVID-19 shut down several states in mid-March. By April 1, the news reported that many Americans could not afford to pay rent. That was only one paycheck. This is a huge problem.

Many community colleges and churches offer free or low-cost financial management programs. Departments on Aging often offer these programs for seniors; caregivers can learn sound principles for themselves as these programs help senior finances improve. Although you can download one of the many financial management tools available on the Internet to start your financial plan, professional advice is invaluable. Contact the Certified Financial Planner Board (www.cfp.net) or one of the other national organizations that certify financial planners (like the National Foundation for Credit Counseling [NFCC, www.nfcc.org] or the National Association of Personal Financial Advisors [NAPFA, www.napfa.org]) to find a qualified advisor. Many professionals recommend working with a certified advisor who charges clients one fee for advice and another for managing the investment plan. They advise against working with planners who also earn commissions from the sale of specific investment products. Earning commissions from product sales can create a conflict of interest; the advisor's potential personal financial gain could affect decisions that should protect your interests. Do your homework before you commit to any financial planning relationship.

*Protect Your Assets: Invest in Age-Appropriate Insurance*

Do not spend a major portion of your income on eldercare unless you have:

- **Health insurance** One emergency room visit can cost an uninsured person thousands of dollars. A hospital visit can cost tens of thousands. Health care debt is the number one cause of bankruptcy in the US. Make sure you have coverage.

- **Disability insurance** protects your most important asset: the income that makes all other assets possible.

- **Homeowner's or renter's** insurance can replace your home and valuables. It also protects your assets if someone gets injured on your property. When you rent, your landlord's insurance covers the building, not your belongings. Carry your own insurance.

- **Car insurance** protects against damage or injury to your car and liability from damage and injury to other drivers and property.

- **Burial** plans cover your funeral expenses. Yes, young adults, even you need to consider this. A financial planner can help you decide whether you need a small life insurance policy, specific burial insurance, or another investment strategy to cover this unexpected need. You do not want to burden your family with these expenses.

- **Life Insurance** becomes a consideration as soon as you have dependents who would suffer financial loss on your death. You may want to leave funds to pay off a home and ease the financial burden on your surviving spouse. You may want to support children's education or care for aged parents when you are not there to meet their needs. There are different types of policies and each type has a different impact on your overall financial plan. Again, the advice of a financial professional is critical.

- **Long-term Care (LTC) Insurance** supports care that Medicare and other health insurance plans do not cover. This may include out-of-pocket deductibles and copayments for health insurance contracts, home care that does not require skilled nurses, assisted-living, as well as adult day services. Some LTC insurance policies also cover care coordination services.

Many financial advisors recommend that people make LTC insurance a priority around age fifty-five. Younger adults might pay more in premiums than they would ever use for LTC. Over age sixty, health challenges may make adults ineligible for coverage. Also, because insurance companies believe that older adults are more likely to submit claims, they usually assess larger premiums for older clients.

LTC insurance companies also base premiums on the predicted growth of the senior population, life expectancy (how long the average person in that age group lives), and projected healthcare costs. However, like everyone else, these companies have no way to anticipate the actual numbers. Many insurance companies underestimated the resources they would need to satisfy claims and remain profitable. Therefore, the number of long-term care insurance companies is decreasing. For many that remain, premiums are skyrocketing while benefits decrease.

Still, this investment is worth investigating and there may be other ways to purchase it. Insurance needs change over the lifespan. Once your dependents become independent or pass away, they will not need your income so life insurance may be less important. Disability insurance may be less relevant once you retire to live on a pension with no active income to protect. At these later life stages, you and your financial advisor may find it prudent to shift some life or disability insurance costs into LTC insurance premiums.

Some financial planners recommend investing money privately, rather than paying any LTC insurance premiums at all. Others advise clients to use the cash value in life insurance policies to pay for long-term care, understanding that this strategy may leave less for beneficiaries.

Professional advice is essential for investing your resources wisely. Instead of relying on companies that sell only insurance, discuss your insurance needs with a certified financial planner who can review your total plan: income, budgeting, debt management, credit status, investing, wealth building, retirement planning, and insurance.

### DO Investigate Tax Benefits for Caregivers

I am grateful to Renee K. Collins, CPA, of RKC Financial Services, Inc. (Flossmoor, IL) for this general information. Tax laws change frequently. *These statements were current at the time I wrote this section and may not be accurate later.* Neither Ms. Collins nor I intend that this information should replace the counsel of your personal financial consultant and we assume no liability for the decisions you make. Please base your decisions and actions on the advice of a certified professional who understands the current requirements, the laws in your state, and your specific situation.

*Do You Qualify for Tax Benefits?*

Before caregivers can receive eldercare tax benefits, seniors must meet Internal Revenue Service (IRS) criteria for dependency and levels of support.

In 2019, to establish dependency, seniors must:

- Be legal residents of the United States (born, naturalized, or permanent residents).
- Have an income less than $3,950 per year, including all forms of taxable income (social security benefits, pensions, dividends, interest, royalties).
- Not file a joint tax returns with spouses unless no taxes are due.
- Not appear as a dependent on anyone else's tax return.

If several siblings participate in the care, only one can claim dependency benefits. Parents are the only dependent seniors who can have a separate residence. Others must share a home with the caregiver.

Caregivers must prove that they provide more than fifty percent of the senior's total expenses including:

- Clothing
- Education
- Entertainment
- Food
- Hired caregivers and adult day programs
- Housekeeping and repairs
- Housing (rent or mortgage, taxes, and insurance)
- Insurance premiums (burial, health, life, long-term care)
- Medical and dental expenses not covered by insurance (including copayments and deductibles)
- Recreation
- Travel

There may be other tax benefits, which will require the same dependency determination.

*The Medical Expense Deduction*

Caregivers can claim deductions for a dependent senior's medical expenses and theirs when the amount not covered by insurance reaches a certain percentage of their adjusted gross income. This amount may change yearly. Common qualifying medical expenses include ambulances, bandages, copayments and deductibles, dental care and doctor visits, eyeglasses, health insurance premiums, hearing aids, prescription drugs, and certain long-term care services.

**Less Obvious Possible Deductions:**
- Adapters to TV sets, telephones, doorbells, smoke alarms, security systems, and other supportive equipment for the hearing and visually impaired
- Assisted-living facilities
- Fees for weight-loss and fitness programs that address obesity-specific diseases (diabetes, sleep apnea and others). Your physician must document that these programs were medically necessary and that you have met all requirements.

- Home care and care coordination services that do not require skilled nurses

- Home modifications to accommodate physical disabilities that meet American Disabilities Act [ADA] standards

### Flexible Spending Account (FSA) or Flex-Ben Accounts

Many companies offer these benefits as part of human resource packages. Every pay period, working caregivers can set aside a certain amount of money from their gross (pre-tax) incomes. This decreases taxable income and creates a fund to reimburse out-of-pocket payments for health, childcare, or other dependent care services (which can include eldercare). Depending on your tax bracket, this program can provide a twenty to thirty-five percent tax saving if you meet the following requirements:

- The dependent must meet IRS criteria.

- The employee must submit invoices that document payment for services. These receipts must include tax identification or social security numbers for the businesses or people you pay. Informal arrangements (like paying unreported cash to family members) will not qualify.

- Employees should be careful to estimate yearly expenses when they decide on the amount of pre-tax money to put aside. Though some programs roll over unused funds to the next year, some will forfeit some or all money that remains in the account after December 31.

In the past, money spent on eldercare did not qualify for Flex-Ben accounts unless caregivers could prove that they provided at least fifty-one percent of seniors' *income.* Even if a senior's income is minimal, most of it comes from Social Security or pensions, not from the caregiver. This made caregivers ineligible for Flex-Ben programs, no matter how much money they spent on the senior's upkeep.

Recently, accountants have begun to use the total cost of a senior's upkeep, not just his income. By including the costs of hired care, medicine, transportation, housing, and other needs, it might be possible for a caregiver to claim more than half of the senior's expenses. To avoid fees and penalties, be careful to speak with a financial advisor who is aware of the laws that govern these policies. In any case, better access to Flex-Ben accounts could make a big difference.

If you decide to claim any of these tax benefits, prepare for a possible audit by keeping complete records. In addition to ALL invoices and receipts, keep track of referrals, prescriptions, and supportive letters from your healthcare professional (including specific diagnosis codes). This information will help you prove that you paid for medically necessary services. Tax laws are extensive, confusing, and always changing. The services of a qualified tax professional are essential.

## DO Plan For Your Future: Make Your Twilight Years Truly Golden

Baby Boomers' retirement planning has been challenging because of stock market losses and confusion about the best strategy for investing in employer-based retirement plans. There have also been frightening headlines about employers that borrow from retirement plans and do not repay the debt or otherwise fail to fund the plans adequately. You need sound financial guidance about retirement investing. Though many churches, libraries, local colleges, and community centers offer financial management classes at little or no cost, professional advice is well worth the money. Again, search for certified professionals who work on a fee-only basis instead of earning commissions from selling specific products. Some financial professionals set consultation fees on a sliding scale based on income.

Research certification requirements and the credentials of the professionals you choose. Ask your accountant or attorney for referrals. Check with the Certified Financial Planner Board (www.cfp.net) or another national organization that certifies financial planners like the National Foundation for Credit Counseling (NFCC): www.nfcc.org, or NAPFA: www.napfa.org.

## DO Lighten Your Children's Load

*Wills and Trusts*

Each state has its own laws about what happens to the property of a person that dies "intestate" (without a will). Investigate the laws in your state. You may find yourself dissatisfied with how and to whom the state would distribute your property after your death (and after your state takes a huge chunk of it!) Avoid being voiceless in this process by preparing a will to explain how you want your assets divided. If your family has generational wealth (money and property intended for transfer to future generations) or you are worried about inheritance taxes for your heirs, work to shelter your assets in the appropriate type of trust. Attorneys and estate planners will help.

## Advance Directives

Wills determine what happens when you die; advance directives determine what happens if you don't. These documents tell your family and physicians how you would choose to manage your health care if you were alive, yet too ill to communicate. Some documents allow you to choose an advocate to make decisions on your behalf. The document also includes your instructions so the advocate knows what you want. We will discuss this further when we consider decision-making at the end of life *(See Chapter 16: End-of-Life Care).*

Do not forget to tell your advocates how to find your important papers (wills, insurance policies, deeds, mortgages, titles, incorporation papers, and other business documents). If you use a safe-deposit box, make sure your representative has permission to open it. Some people worry that their advocates might abuse power and take control while they are still able to make decisions. To ease this fear, have your lawyer add language that requires your advocate to show proof of your disability (for example, a physician's statement) before taking control.

Many families are reluctant to discuss wills, trusts, advance directives, and funeral arrangements. However, if you have these discussions, the people you choose to handle your affairs will feel less guilty when they have to take responsibility. They will also have fewer fights with other family members when everyone knows they are following *your* directions.

\*\*\*\*\*\*\*\*\*\*\*\*\*\*\*\*\*\*\*\*\*\*\*\*\*\*

My mother prepared power of attorney documents long before dementia took her from us. She told my brother and me, "One day, I may be too sick to take care of myself. I want you to know that I trust you to do what's best for me. No matter what I might say at the time, I raised you; I know who you are, and I trust you."

\*\*\*\*\*\*\*\*\*\*\*\*\*\*\*\*\*\*\*\*\*\*\*\*\*\*

Our mother's words and the documents she prepared comforted us and lessened our guilt as we made the hard decisions in her care plan. Prepare your advance directives. discuss your wishes with your children and give them that same comfort.

Though Mother gave my brother and me joint powers of attorney, and it worked for us, I do not recommend this strategy. Even the closest siblings can disagree under stress, and this can paralyze care plans. I recommend designating one person as power of attorney to make decisions for you when you cannot. Be sure to designate alternate advocates in case the person you choose decides not to accept the responsibility or is unable to do so. In most states, powers of attorney for finance require legal advice while health care powers of attorney do not. Even so, legal advice is always helpful.

*****************************

### DO Grow Up; *Meet Your Own Financial Needs*

If you have relied on a senior's assets or income, please, start taking care of yourself today. If you don't do this, you will be crippled when your seniors pass on.

Though times are hard, community colleges are important resources for your job search. They often partner with local chambers of commerce to host job fairs and other networking opportunities. Most of these services are free. If you have education and skills, many community colleges offer career counseling. They will help you buff up your resume, strengthen your interviewing skills, search potential employer databases, and make the most of social media in your job search. If you want to start a business, some community colleges have small-business think-tanks to help with business plans, organization, governance, equipment, accounting, finances, marketing, human resources, and applications for small business loans. If you need to become more marketable, many community colleges also offer time-efficient, less expensive ways to earn certifications that can improve your chances of finding employment.

If you are business-wardrobe-challenged, many communities maintain business attire closets to help. Goodwill, the Salvation Army, and other community organizations offer affordable, gently used business suits, shirts and ties, blouses, shoes, and even briefcases.

If you have a disability, contact the Department of Disability Services in your state to learn about benefits that apply to you. If you are a veteran, check with the VA; it has resources for counseling, employment, housing, medical care, and other types of support.

DO NOT *Think They Owe You Anything*

I have met people who believe caregiving earns them free access to a senior's assets. You are entitled to reimburse yourself when you spend your own money for their upkeep, but you may not use seniors' funds for ANYTHING that does not directly pertain to their care. If you do, you are guilty of elder abuse, in the category of financial exploitation. You can go to jail.

Some eldercare agencies will hire family members, train them, and assign them to their own seniors (possibly along with other clients). Instead of believing that your seniors *owe* you a living, become a professional and earn your living.

DO NOT *Depend on Your Senior's Income or Allow Your Children to Do So*

In more than thirty years of practice, I have seen seniors without enough money to fund their care because they spent (and continue to spend) it on younger adults.

\*\*\*\*\*\*\*\*\*\*\*\*\*\*\*\*\*\*\*\*\*\*\*\*\*

- Instead of retiring as planned, an eighty-four-year-old was still working full-time to continue more than ten years of monthly mortgage payments for a "child" who is of sound mind and body, not under the influence of any drug, and has an advanced degree.

- A couple paid for their daughter's education through graduate school. When they were in their late sixties, their daughter was a thirty-four-year-old single mother. Though the daughter was employed in her field, her parents subsidized her condo and car. They also paid childcare expenses for their six-year-old granddaughter.

  The daughter became angry when her parents gave her brother a loan to expand his successful social media business and would not invest in her plan to start making hand-painted baseball caps to sell at local craft fairs. She demanded the money and when her parents asked to see her business plan, she cursed them for "being in my business."

- An eighty-year-old woman and her sixty-year-old daughter lived in a house that the mother owned outright. Her thirty-five-year-old grandson convinced his mother and grandmother to take out a second mortgage to finance his new music business. He swore he would repay the loan. He had no business experience and no talent. When his business folded, he hopped into the BMW his mother and grandmother had helped him buy and moved to another state. His mother worked as a minimum-wage greeter in a big-box store. Her lack of skills and poor health made it impossible for her to find a better job. Even with her mother's Social Security check, the women were unable to make the mortgage payments. Facing homelessness, they applied for subsidized senior housing with a six-month waiting list. That young man's mother and grandmother had to share a sofa bed in a relative's basement until a unit became available.

*************************

Many seniors earned and saved money, paid for their property, and managed their investments. These resources should be available to secure the rest of their lives yet younger adults often live a lifestyle the seniors purchase. They stay in the seniors' homes for free, enjoy their food, phone, car, electronics, Internet, and other costly resources without contributing to the household. They may also demand that the senior subsidize their lifestyles outside the home.

Recall the young woman whose parents did not rush to subsidize the crafting business she proposed after they had paid for her education and housing and helped with her child. She was angry because she couldn't get even *more* resources from her parents! *Why was it okay for her to ask them out of her business, but it was not okay for them to ask her out of their pockets?*

I have heard some younger adults say their parents are going to leave them everything anyway so why not get it now? They don't realize, or don't care that their spending can make the seniors uncomfortable and insecure while they are alive. Many of these younger adults don't consider whether they could support these seniors should a need arise after the money is gone.

Even if you are giving care, it is criminal to take money from your seniors or use their credit and other resources for yourself without their permission and without any coercion. However, in many cases, this kind of mistreatment could not occur if the seniors did not allow it. Many seniors are accustomed to supporting younger loved ones. They will hurt themselves to continue that support even when the younger adults should be able to care for themselves. (*See Chapter 11: Protect Your Emotional*

*Health, Are You Codependent?*)

Still, I appeal to younger adults. Even if the seniors give permission or offer, step up and take care of yourself. Younger adults are not entitled to support themselves on the backs of their seniors. If you do that, *how can you say, "I'm grown?"*

Financial health is a critical factor in caregiver survival. Manage your finances today, plan for tomorrow, and make all adults stand on their own two feet. These strategies will decrease the financial stress that can cause family strife and insecurity in retirement. Good financial management can also avoid conditions that erode your sense of well-being, and lead to anxiety, depression, other emotional turmoil.

# CHAPTER 11

# Protect Your Emotional Health: *The Mind You Save May Be Your Own*

Caregiving can dry up emotional reserves because fear, insecurity, and guilt take a great toll on caregivers. Isolation, anger, and fatigue make these feelings more powerful and can lead to depression.

In the second section, we discussed ways to avoid fear and anxiety by identifying the senior's needs and working out the care plan. There are also ways to manage other factors that threaten a caregiver's emotional state.

## Avoid Guilt

You will be a better caregiver and a healthier one when you refuse to let guilt sap your energy. These strategies will help you avoid guilt and its impact on your emotional health.

\*\*\*\*\*\*\*\*\*\*\*\*\*\*\*\*\*\*\*\*\*\*\*\*\*

Ms. Price had two school-age children and a ninety-minute round-trip commute every day. Between her work schedule, childcare, and her children's activities, she could visit her mom in the nursing home only two or three times a week. Ms. Price talked to the nurses regularly and arranged her schedule so she could attend every care conference. She also traded visits with her sister-in-law and a couple of trusted friends to ensure that someone spent time with Mom on the days Ms. Price couldn't visit. When she did visit, Ms. Price read her mom's favorite bible stories, sang her favorite hymns, or played recordings of the musicians Mom loved. Even so, Ms. Price was heartbroken because she could not be at the nursing home every day.

In addition to being a good daughter, Ms. Price was a good mother; she made an event of every moment she spent with her kids. On Mondays and Wednesdays, they had breakfast together; on Tuesdays and Thursdays, they shared dinner. On Fridays, she and the kids made tacos or pizza, popped popcorn, and watched a video together. They also had a special dinner every Sunday. Ms. Price tried to get to every game or recital but again, she traded off with other family members or friends who knew the kids well.

Ms. Price also made time for herself. She had breakfast with her girlfriends on Saturday mornings while the kids did chores and went out with other friends two Saturday evenings each month.

\*\*\*\*\*\*\*\*\*\*\*\*\*\*\*\*\*\*\*\*\*\*\*\*\*

Ms. Price had many opportunities to feel guilty. She could have wrung her hands and cried about how she let everyone down. Instead, she made the most of each minute.

- Even though she could not have every meal with her children, she made every meal special.

- Instead of beating herself up for being unable to see her mother every day, she remembered the Third and Fourth Keys to Caregiver Survival. She told her friends she needed help and she let them help. (See *Chapter 8: Get Help from Family and Friends, The Five Keys to Caregiver Survival.*)

- She could have refused to make time for herself. Instead, she remembered the Second and Fifth Keys to Caregiver Survival. She knew there wasn't an "S" on her chest and realized it was okay to get help. She also put her mask on first and arranged time for fun so she could stay strong and give better care.

Ms. Price accepted that she could not do it all; she did what she could and pulled a team together for everything else. Even though she wasn't giving everybody *everything*, she knew she was doing her best.

*Give Yourself Credit When You Do a Good Job*

Many caregivers love their seniors and acknowledge that the seniors made them who they are. These caregivers are grateful and want to do right by their elders. However, many also fear that they are not honoring their seniors and are terrified that they are *not* doing what is right. Before they succumb to emotional distress, these caregivers should take another look.

\*\*\*\*\*\*\*\*\*\*\*\*\*\*\*\*\*\*\*\*\*\*\*\*\*

My pastor honored me by letting me take care of his mother. In the three years I served as her doctor, Mama Carolyn declined from moderate to severe dementia, and Pastor Mike and his family continued to care for her at home. In one office visit, Pastor Mike said he often angered his mother by jumping up to help her before she needed help and by rushing to protect her before she did anything dangerous. As we talked about easing up a bit, it became clear that Pastor Mike's greatest fear was that he wasn't a good caregiver. He could not bear to think that something would happen to his mother as he said, "on my watch."

I asked him when Mama Carolyn had last:

- Been in the emergency room or a hospital
- Been hungry, dirty, cold, too hot, or otherwise uncomfortable
- Gone without medical care because her caregivers failed to contact her doctor immediately when there was a change or a question
- Had a fall, a broken bone, an infection, or any unmet needs
- Missed a doctor's appointment
- Suffered wounds or any other injuries
- Seemed unhappy instead of cheery

Pastor Mike not only denied that any of this had ever happened, he seemed appalled at the thought. I told him, and I'm telling you: *THAT'S GOOD CAREGIVING.*

If you have:

✓ Met with the doctors and received the LOCRx

✓ Pulled your team together and given the recommended care in the appropriate care site

✓ Acted quickly to get the information you needed whenever there was a new problem or question,

✓ Continually worked to meet your senior's needs as promptly as possible,

*YOU ARE A GOOD CAREGIVER!*


**Remember**:

Guilt hurts you without helping your loved ones. Take steps to work through this emotion by getting the information you need to do your best. Then fix any actions that need to improve and give yourself credit for doing what you could.


**Avoid Disappointment:** *Don't Lean on Reeds*

Laurie Beth Jones wrote a book called *Jesus in Blue Jeans.* Each chapter describes traits in Jesus' personality that could lead to fuller lives for everyone, regardless of faith or spiritual orientation.[24] In the chapter "*He Did Not Lean on Reeds*," Ms. Jones cautions us to stop relying on people who are repeatedly unreliable.

*************************

Mr. Ellis has three daughters who live at opposite corners of a triangle that covers the metropolitan area. Rhonda is the middle daughter. She and her own daughters (Mr. Ellis' granddaughters) take turns caring for him without any help from Rhonda's sisters. The oldest sister has a hectic work schedule. The youngest sister is so upset about their father's illness that she admits, "I can't handle this."

Whenever caregiving options arise, instead of making the distance convenient for her and her daughters, Rhonda always looks for resources in the center of the region. She wants to "make it easier for all of us to get to him." Then, she gets angry because she travels a long distance to visit Mr. Ellis while the others "don't even come to see about Dad."

Rhonda plays out this cycle with every new care decision and burns herself out in the process.

\*\*\*\*\*\*\*\*\*\*\*\*\*\*\*\*\*\*\*\*\*\*\*\*\*

Rhonda is leaning on reeds. Her problem isn't that her sisters won't participate in the care plan. Rhonda's problem is that she keeps *expecting* them to participate. She could save herself disappointment, anger, and stress if she would accept that her sisters are not going to do what she wants them to do. Instead, she should arrange her dad's care in a way that is convenient for her and her daughters: the people who provide the care.

When people prove themselves unreliable, *stop relying on them.* Start working with social service professionals to find resources and get the job done in ways that are most convenient for YOU. If people don't like it, refer to the *"Show Up or Shut Up"* section of *Chapter 8: Get Help from Family and Friends.*

## Avoid Regrets: *Keep Your "I LOVE YOUs" up to date*

We met Ms. Price earlier in this chapter, in the section *You Can Only Do What You Can Do.* She made special time for her kids, her mom, and herself. Ms. Price kept her "I LOVE YOUs" up to date and so can you.

Even if you do not have a lot of time, give your best in special ways. You can maintain cherished relationships by making calls, leaving messages, sending cards, e-mails, video messages, or texts. Be creative. I know a caregiver who has a fifteen-minute conference call for prayer with her friends at 6 a.m. every Thursday morning. Now that Skype, Zoom, FaceTime, and other digital programs allow people to talk and see each other, it is easier to give the gift of "presence" even when you can't be present. (Thanks to Rev. Gloria Randolph of Giving God the Glory Ministries, who introduced me to the gift-of-presence-concept).

Keep your "I LOVE YOUs" up to date and regrets will not add to your grief when your loved ones are gone. We never know which one of us will be the next to make that transition. Let everyone know how you feel now in case it's the last time.

### Don't Be Afraid to Make a New Plan: *It's Okay to Change Lanes When You Get a Clue*

Sometimes, circumstances force you to change course. No matter what you've decided in the past, don't feel guilty if new information or a change in resources dictates a new route. When you change direction to give the best care, you are finding another way to say, "I love you."

\*\*\*\*\*\*\*\*\*\*\*\*\*\*\*\*\*\*\*\*\*\*\*\*\*\*\*

Earlier in her mother's illness, Ms. Price had said "never" to nursing home placement. However, Ms. Price realized there was no way to work, raise her children, and meet her mom's increasing care needs at home. The nursing home was the best option. (*See Chapter 15: The Nursing Home Decision: When You Promised "Never"—Honor the Spirit of the Promise*)

\*\*\*\*\*\*\*\*\*\*\*\*\*\*\*\*\*\*\*\*\*\*\*\*\*\*\*

### Don't Whine. Hum: *Say "No" to Self-Pity*

Another chapter in Laurie Beth Jones' book *Jesus in Blue Jeans* is "He Didn't Whine; He Hummed."[25] Some caregivers whine, as if they want to tell everyone, "See how hard I'm working? See how much I've sacrificed?" These caregivers need to recognize that they *chose* the caregiving role.

\*\*\*\*\*\*\*\*\*\*\*\*\*\*\*\*\*\*\*\*\*\*\*\*\*\*\*

Karla had been the primary caregiver for her dad for three years. When she was growing up, her father openly preferred her two brothers and ignored his daughter. He never supported her and seemed to take no notice when she moved out of the house. Karla felt abandoned.

When her father became ill, the brothers planned nursing home placement. Karla refused to allow it. She quit her job and moved back home to care for her dad. She called her brothers frequently to cry that she had given up her dreams and her life to care for their father even though she knew he did not love her. She took every opportunity to say the same thing to her dad.

One evening, neighbors heard yelling and a loud crash. They called the police. Her father had pushed Karla into a bookcase and she had shoved back. The police contacted Adult Protective Services (APS). Fortunately, in that state, law enforcement worked closely with social services. APS social workers found adult day services for her dad and counseling for Karla.

The counselors helped Karla realize that she had moved back home to make her father see that she was a good child who deserved his love instead of neglect or contempt. Through counseling, Karla accepted that she could never earn her dad's approval and it was not because she didn't deserve it; he was incapable of giving it. She learned that whining to her brothers would not get their sympathy or their help. She also realized that whining to her father made things worse.

Karla made an active decision to continue as her dad's caregiver. She continued in counseling and felt more empowered. While her father used adult day services, Karla went back to school to begin a new career. She cared for him every night and took advantage of respite care services when she needed to be away. As she became more patient and less needy in her interactions with her dad, he became less agitated.

Her dad has now passed on. Karla works as a medical biller and feels good about having developed into an excellent caregiver.

* * * * * * * * * * * * * * * * * * * * * * * *

Many caregivers say, "I have no choice; nobody else will do it." In fact, there was a choice. Other family members chose *not* to do it, right? You chose the other route.

Most of you are not legal guardians. Even if you are a spouse or there are no other family members, you are not *legally* obligated to provide care. (This will vary from state to state for investigations of elder abuse and neglect).

You *chose* to be the caregiver. Instead of feeling like a victim, see yourself as a victor. Embrace your choice to give care. Instead of whining, hum and mmmmotor on, like a well-oiled machine. Find out what you need to do (LOCRx) and work with social service professionals to get the help you need. Take care of yourself and keep doing the job well.

## You Don't Have to Like Caregiving: *Tell the Truth, At Least to Yourself*

It's okay to dislike caregiving. It's even okay to dislike your seniors. It's okay to admit that you're angry, resentful, and feel like you're drowning. What you feel does not have to dictate what you do. You can continue to give great care despite acknowledging these feelings. In fact, it is dangerous to deny or ignore them. When you try to bury these emotions, you compress them and make them powerful enough to overwhelm you. These feelings always come out eventually$_{(26)}$ though they do not always explode. Sometimes, they ooze into your voice as you argue with co-workers or snap at the people you love.

✱✱✱✱✱✱✱✱✱✱✱✱✱✱✱✱✱✱✱✱✱✱✱✱✱✱✱✱✱✱✱✱

Mrs. O'Bannon's eighty-three-year-old mother suffered from severe arthritis and congestive heart failure. The energy required to walk on painful and deformed knees was too much for Mom's heart. Although she was in a wheelchair, she could get to the bathroom and take a sandwich out of the fridge.

Mrs. O'Bannon was an only child; she was fifty-four years old, married, had independent adult children, and she had a high-stress job as an insurance executive. After a long day at work, her second shift began. Most nights, she went to her mother's home to bring groceries, make meals, and help write checks to pay bills. She also spent most weekends with her mom cleaning and doing laundry. Mrs. O'Bannon rarely went out with her husband or her friends, and she had not had a manicure in months.

Mrs. O'Bannon's husband always handled the evening meal but his wife rarely sat at the dinner table with him. She would run in from her mom's house, grab a plate, and rush to her home office to work on one of the many job-related projects she managed.

At one point, an upcoming performance evaluation raised Mrs. O'Bannon's stress level. She was so focused on an important project that she barely ate. She rushed her visits with her mother and worked at home into the early morning hours. One evening, her mother asked her to stay a little longer and Mrs. O'Bannon yelled, "What more do you want from me? I already spend more time here than I do in my own house!" Mom matched her daughter's screaming and said, "Well, don't do me no favors!" Mrs. O'Bannon stormed out. She walked into her home and right into her office with body language that seemed to broadcast, "Speak to me and DIE!" Her husband did not say a word.

Later, as Mrs. O'Bannon microwaved a cup of coffee, she felt guilty about screaming at her mom. As she picked up the phone to apologize, Mrs. O'Bannon noticed that her husband had not remembered to take out the trash. She slammed down the phone and snatched up the bag, which burst and spewed garbage all over the kitchen floor. When her husband rushed in to see why his wife was yelling, she asked him why he enjoyed making her life so hard. He left the kitchen without a word.

At her performance evaluation, Mrs. O'Bannon's boss rated the quality of her work as outstanding though he said, "The human resource department has taken several official complaints from your staff. It seems that you threw a file at someone and slammed a book on a desk hard enough to spill coffee. I'm sorry. I will have to put an official warning in your permanent file. If there is no improvement in thirty days, you will lose a week's pay and have to attend anger management classes."

That evening, Mrs. O'Bannon and her husband sent two e-mails: one to an eldercare consultant and the other to their doctor, requesting a referral for behavioral health counseling.

*******************************

Feelings are neither good nor bad; they just are. Related actions can be positive or negative, yet as I said, feelings do not have to control your actions. To continue to be a good caregiver, you will have to work through anger, resentment, and the sense that you are well beyond the end of your rope. Unexpressed feelings can hurt you physically by eroding your sleep or making you overeat or overspend. By increasing the level of chronic stress, these buried feelings may also increase your risk of accidents and stress-related illnesses (like addictions, heart disease, and even some cancers). They can also interfere with work performance and hurt people around you.

Find a useful, safe place to tell the truth. This is not whining or humming; it's preventive maintenance. It may not be a good idea to confide in family members, especially if family relationships add drama. It is never a good idea to confide in the seniors in your care. They are dealing with their own fears and disappointments about being disabled. They do not need added pressure, sadness, or guilt from you. An objective professional is a better choice.

Behavioral health professionals can help you deal more effectively with feelings you might express with hurtful behaviors. They can also help you move these feelings into areas of your mind and heart where they won't do as much emotional damage. This keeps the feelings from seeping out to cause actions that interfere with your relationships or undermine caregiving.

### Getting Behavioral Health Counseling Isn't a Weakness

When your car isn't running well, do you always fix it yourself? Do you rebuild the engine, knock out all the dents, and touch up the paint? Even if the car is running well, don't you still get the oil changed and check the tire pressure and brakes? Given unlimited time and the right manuals, we could probably do everything our cars need, but why would we? Trained professionals fill those roles and free up our time and energy for other important activities. Try to look at behavioral health counselors the same way you look at auto mechanics and other paid professionals. Seeing a counselor doesn't mean you are crazy or weak. Even if you are still functioning well, stress can make caregiving cost too much emotionally. If you had nothing else to do with your time, you could probably work through your guilt, sadness, anger, and other hurtful emotions by yourself, but that is not a good use of your time. Find a skilled behavioral health professional and get on with your life.

### Medicine for the Mind

*Depression* is a common response to caregiver stress, yet this condition is not a weakness either. For some people, depression follows particularly stressful situations. Others are at risk because there an imbalance in levels of neurotransmitters in their brains. (Neurotransmitters are chemicals that brain and other nerve cells use to talk to each other.)

While some people with depression respond to counseling alone, others benefit from medicine. Many people worry about becoming "addicted" to antidepressant medicine. Ask yourself, "Are people with diabetes *addicted* to the medicines that control their blood sugar? Are people with hypertension *addicted* to their blood pressure medicine?" No. People with diabetes and hypertension need a chemical adjustment. When depression interferes with their lives, people need a chemical adjustment. There are many options for medicines that are safe and effective under the supervision of a skilled primary care physician or psychiatrist. Some people need antidepressant medicine for only a short time; others have relapses between medicine-free years. Still others need medicine continuously for the rest of their lives. In any case, these medicines are usually more successful when coupled with behavioral health counseling.

Depression is a physical ailment, not a character flaw. It does not mean you are crazy. Depression is a medical condition like diabetes or hypertension. Get help.

*Anxiety* is another response to the stress of caregiving. Anti-anxiety medicine (anxiolytics) can be addictive and cause physical cravings for the medicine even when the anxiety has passed. There may also be dangerous physical signs of withdrawal when you stop the medicine or lower the dose too quickly. Because of the addiction-risk, most health professionals recommend anxiolytics for short-term therapy only. Also note that many antidepressants have positive effects on anxiety without the physical addiction of traditional anxiolytics. Professionals also recommend counseling, cognitive behavioral therapy (CBT), self-calming techniques, mindfulness, and other stress-management strategies. In some cases, these behavioral adjustments can decrease the need for long-term medicine. Still, if your doctor recommends medicine, don't be afraid to take it. Discuss how long you should expect to use the medicine, the counseling and behavioral techniques that might decrease your need for it, and how you will gradually decrease its use. If you are one of the people who need long-term anti-depressants, remember the people with diabetes and high blood pressure. You need to control your condition just as they do. When non-medication strategies don't bring enough control, life-long medicine is the key to staying healthy. Work with your doctor to find the best treatment plan for you.

### Are you Codependent?

Many of the stories in this book show caregivers that move beyond healthy caregiving and risk codependency.

The term "codependent" grew out of "co-alcoholic," which described people who ignored, excused, enabled, tried to justify, or control the behavior of alcoholics. The codependent's happiness depends on the alcoholic's happiness and he feels responsible for the alcoholic's recovery. Codependents use all their energy to take care of others and forget to take care of themselves. They often deny that they need help and refuse to let others take care of them. (Does any of this sound familiar?)

Some professionals believe codependency is a compulsive behavior that underlies all addictions and other compulsive behaviors. One person can never fully control another person's behavior. When hurtful or scary behaviors persist, the codependent may see this as a personal failure and try to numb the pain with substance abuse, eating disorders, gambling, shopping, risky sexual activity, and other destructive behaviors. The pain-numbing addictive behavior can persist long after the relationship ends. It can also pollute other relationships.

Codependency can describe any relationship in which one person over-functions and moves into the responsibility-space of someone who under-functions. Codependent relationships can be romantic unions, platonic friendships, and even interactions in the workplace. Family connections can be especially challenging and the parent-child relationship is vulnerable, in both directions.

Young children can take emotional responsibility for a parent with an addiction, physical, mental, or emotional illness. Sometimes, these kids take over operational responsibilities, as well. They get themselves to school, do laundry, cook, shop, and even interact with creditors. Parents can take responsibility for a child's homework, write college application essays, and intervene in teen and young adult relationships. Older parents risk retirement funds and financial stability to rescue younger adults who "fail to launch." Caregivers can blur the boundaries between healthy caregiving and codependency when they risk their health and financial security, endure social isolation and abuse, sacrifice their joy, and drain themselves in eldercare.

The RESOURCES list at the back of this book includes information to help you decide whether codependency is an issue for you. If you believe you are at risk, these resources will help you identify unhealthy relationships and find help to move into recovery. With this support, you can stop enabling, put everyone's needs and responsibilities into proper perspective, and learn to take care of yourself.

Your emotional health is as important as your physical and financial well-being. Guard it carefully, and do not forget to nurture the deeper wells of strength in your spirit.

# CHAPTER 12

## Protect Your Spiritual Health: *Put on the Armor of Peace; Wield the Sword of Forgiveness*

Caregiver survival depends on a strong inner spirit that protects itself from despair. This kind of spirit finds joyful purpose, sees the big picture, avoids guilt, and knows when to let go. This spirit is also strong enough to forgive.

### Find Joy Outside of Caregiving: *Make Time to Do Something You Love*

You are more than a caregiver. You will be a better caregiver if you nurture the other parts of your life.

\*\*\*\*\*\*\*\*\*\*\*\*\*\*\*\*\*\*\*\*\*\*\*\*\*\*\*

Ms. Allen loves to bowl in a community league and sing in her church choir. She frees up time by using adult day services and by working with respite volunteers from her church to help take care of her mother.

Mr. Nelson cares for his grandmother and uses an adult day center with early evening and weekend hours so he can study Taekwondo twice a week after work. On Saturday morning, he teaches the martial art to kids at a youth center. He has also pulled together a business team to help him open his own Taekwondo school.

Mr. Reardon sings in a barbershop quartet that performs in his community and at his wife's nursing home. Weather permitting, he takes Mrs. Reardon out to lunch, to afternoon concerts, and seminars at the local library. He also mentors troubled teenagers.

Mrs. Taylor hires a respite worker to care for her mother two mornings per week. She alternates between taking a yoga class, getting a massage, having coffee with friends, and participating in a book club. Once a year, she makes use of the respite program in an assisted-living community and spends a week enjoying the fall leaves in Michigan.

Joy is filling and contagious. Create some joy. It will spill into other areas of your life and allow you to smile and laugh through your caregiving. Joy also helps you share good vibes with others and give them hope. When struggling caregivers see your joy, they may realize it's possible to create their own joy to help them cope with their challenges.

### "If I Can Help Somebody:" *Find Purpose Outside of Caregiving*

Do you have talents and interests outside of caregiving that could help someone else? Lift your head, look above your misery, and be a blessing to someone outside your situation. I'm not asking you to take on more caregiving, just to share a little sunshine.

If you cannot think of a place to pitch in, please consider mentoring younger people. Today's teens and preteens face challenges most of us have never faced, even as adults. They deal with much more violence and peer pressure than we did as kids. Parents are working themselves to death; grandparents and other family members may be in other parts of the country. Divorce, job transfers, and the increased mobility of our society have eroded the stability of neighborhoods and relationships, leaving kids with fewer resources. Most after-school programs accommodate kids only under age twelve. Many teenagers are without adult supervision for three or four hours every weekday until their parents come home from work. These are the "witching hours" when kids are vulnerable to violence and the consequences of experimenting with alcohol, drugs, and sex.

Even though they have reached legal age, young adults in their twenties and thirties can also benefit from your wisdom and support. Neuroscientists now say the brain continues to develop well into in the twenties. The parts of the brain that make plans, consider consequences before acting, pull together necessary resources, and follow through are still maturing in the young adult years. Older people may not have intimate experience with the specific situations that challenge today's young adults. We do know about the consequences of poor planning and bad decisions; we've already made those mistakes.

Today's difficult economic times also create hardship for young adults that we did not face. A college degree is the new GED. Even though it's almost impossible to find a job without a bachelor's degree, the cost puts college out of reach for many Americans. The job market is difficult and many of the available salaries won't support the American Dream (especially in the face of huge school loans). Because of these factors, it may be easier for these young people to fall and for those that do, it can be harder to get up.

It is also harder because many young adults do not understand the work, patience, and perseverance that life requires. Neither do they understand how failure can empower success. I believe one factor is that the Baby Boomer generation did not allow our kids to fail or even struggle. Though we wanted to be good parents and give them what our parents could not give us, we did not let them see how hard we had to work to make those resources possible. (One of my friends said she never told her son she could not afford something because she did not want him to worry). We also raised them in a success culture that praised and rewarded them for just showing up. I find that many of our young adults are surprised when raises, promotions, and other accolades don't come as quickly as they would like. Many believe the good life happens by magic until the "college of hard knocks" knocks them over.

As today's young adults cope with the realities of adulthood, we cannot overestimate the wisdom and support young people can get from responsible, sane adults. It may be easier for them to hear someone who isn't Mom or Dad. That would be you.

Share your wisdom through a homework hotline or a foster grandparent program. Pitch in and push your community leaders to start afterschool programs for teens. Get involved in mentorship programs for young people of all ages through churches, community organizations, alumni associations, or schools. Many of our young people are discouraged and they are in trouble; they need you.

### "Threads in a Tapestry": *Concentrate on Doing What You Can; You Don't Have to Control Everything*

Regardless of your spiritual orientation, caregiving is easier when you can believe your specific hardship has purpose as part of something bigger. Several years ago, I heard a song called "Threads in a Tapestry." It said that everyone is a thread in the tapestry of life, and each thread has a unique, essential function. As one thread, we can see only our little corner of the tapestry, and that corner might look terrible. The good thing is we just have to be the best thread we can in our little portion. We do not have to understand it all; we're not responsible for all of it. Many caregivers take comfort in believing that a Power sees the whole pattern, understands everything, and ensures that the entire tapestry makes beautiful sense.

### Gain Strength from Your Trials: *"Your Test Becomes Your Testimony; Your Mess Becomes Your Ministry."*

Many wise seniors and spiritual leaders have used this phrase to help people see that good can come from life challenges, and everything happens for a reason. Your testimony is not *that* you survive trouble. Your testimony is *how* you survive with joy and hope. Get your head up above your own misery, share your strength and your story, create some joy, and be a blessing to somebody else.

Again, I am not asking you to take on more direct caregiving responsibility. I just want you to look for joy in your current situation and share it. Despite your grief, can you find something positive for yourself, for your senior, for someone else? Despite the trouble, can you look for the lesson in your situation? That is your testimony. Can you share what you've learned in your struggle? Can that knowledge help another caregiver who is toiling farther back on the road you have already traveled? That is your ministry.

Feeling joy in the face of hardship protects you from despair. When you create joy within yourself, you become resilient. You can work your plan to stay healthy despite the stress and inspire other caregivers to hold on. Then, they also pay that joy forward.

## God Always Answers Prayer; Sometimes the Answer is "NO."

Even when you do everything you can, sometimes things don't work the way you want them to.

*************************

Mr. and Mrs. O'Connor were in their eighties. They lived alone in the large, beautiful home they had maintained with great pride for sixty years. Neither Mr. nor Mrs. O'Connor had any memory problems, and they were both retired postal workers with good pensions. Mrs. O'Connor paid the bills, and Mr. O'Connor managed their portfolio of investments. The O'Connors had two adult children who lived out of town. Their primary support was their niece, Zora who lived in the area. Zora helped with grocery shopping; she drove the seniors to church and took them out for dinner every Sunday. She arranged for teenagers from the church to put the trash out, cut the grass, and shovel the snow.

The O'Connor's health began to decline. Mr. O'Connor developed severe, painful arthritis in his hips, knees, and back. This made it hard for him to walk and take care of his personal needs. Mrs. O'Connor suffered several heart attacks, and each one left her weaker. Shortness of breath and leg swelling kept her in a recliner most of the day and night.

The seniors looked to their niece for more help. When they could no longer negotiate the basement stairs, they called on her to do their laundry. Neither senior could get to the bathroom in time, so the laundry was quite a chore. Within a year, Zora had also shouldered responsibility for housekeeping and taking care of the dogs. She cooked several times each week and provided transportation to doctor appointments for both seniors.

Zora knew her aunt and uncle had a good income. They also had significant equity in their home. Even so, Mrs. O'Connor refused when her niece suggested they hire a housekeeper/companion. "We won't let strangers into our house," Mrs. O'Connor said. "You are our family. We don't trust anybody else."

They also balked at the expense. Zora suggested they apply for a reverse mortgage to get funds to hire the help they needed and Mr. O'Connor said, "The bank will never take my house out from under me." According to

Mrs. O'Connor, that was that.

Zora was in her sixties and had medical problems of her own. She struggled with diabetes and painful arthritis that affected her back and knees. Zora's children visited for Christmas and were shocked that their mother looked so frail. When they asked her to come live with them so they could see to her golden years, Zora refused. She knew her aunt and uncle had no other support. She did agree to try to get more help for the O'Connors.

Zora arranged for the seniors to see a local geriatrician who confirmed that both were of sound mind. The geriatrician recommended a private eldercare consultant to help them arrange in-home help and other services. The O'Connors refused to spend the money. Zora called the local Area Agency on Aging to investigate services that set fees based on income. The O'Connor's income was too high to qualify for free assistance from the state, and even though their copayment would have been less expensive than the private care manager's fee, the seniors refused to pay.

Zora called the O'Connors' children who had busy lives of their own. They said, "Mom and Dad don't need us in their business," they said. "They've been doing everything right for years."

Over the next six months, Zora's back pain got worse. Physical therapy did not work, and pain shots provided only temporary relief. She took so much arthritis medicine that her stomach began to hurt. Her doctor recommended back surgery with a recuperation time of at least six weeks. Zora was sure disaster would strike if she was unavailable to her aunt and uncle for that long. She put off the surgery.

One day, when she was walking down the basement to do the laundry, Zora's left leg became weak and she fell down the stairs. She was lucky there were no broken bones. However, her doctor found that arthritis in her back had pinched the nerves that controlled her leg. If she let the situation continue, the weakness could be permanent. This was the last straw.

Zora hired a realtor to put her house on the market and arranged to move to the town where her children lived. She planned to have her surgery there and stay with her daughter through her recuperation. Once Zora recovered, she would move into a nearby condo. She called the O'Connor's children and told them she planned to leave in one month. She gave them a packet containing contact information for the geriatrician, the eldercare consultant, and the other resources she had collected.

When Zora told her aunt and uncle about her plans, both seniors were furious and said, "After all we've done for you, how can you just walk out on us like this?"

Mr. and Mrs. O'Connor had raised their niece, and she thought of them as her parents. Zora was sorry they were disappointed in her, and it hurt that they thought she was ungrateful. Still, she had her own health to consider, and she told them so.

She reminded her aunt and uncle that they had worked hard, saved their money, and were more than capable of arranging to take care of themselves. Even though she agreed to be present during a visit from the Department on Aging social worker, the O'Connors refused to participate.

Zora stopped doing the laundry and the housekeeping and continued to bring food until the end of the month when she said goodbye and left town. She called once a week to say hello and to answer questions about whom the O'Connors should call for help. She also talked to their children, who had started to get calls from their parents and the neighbors.

No matter what the O'Connors or their children said, Zora did not feel guilty, nor did she come back. Instead of taking their panic to heart, she gave information and empathy. The O'Connor's children had to take leave from their jobs to fly into town for frequent visits. When the seniors realized that neither their niece nor their children would move back home to care for them full-time, the O'Connors finally agreed to hire help.

Zora underwent successful back surgery, and she continues to enjoy the love and support of her family. The O'Connors lived in their home with hired caregivers until they each passed away (two and four years later) in their bed, as they had wished.

*************************

Could Zora have continued to take responsibility for her seniors in the face of her growing back pain? Could she have convinced them to pay for the resources that would relieve her? The answer to both questions was "No."

You did everything you were supposed to do. You did not **deny.** You admitted there was a problem. You did not **delay.** You approached the challenge directly and acted right on time. You did not **despair**. You reached for help and found a care team and the LOCRx. You were specific when you asked your family for help and made the best use of your resources. (*See Chapters 3, 4, and 5*) However, he *still* won't take the medicine; she *still* won't eat properly; they *still* won't cooperate, and family members *still* won't show up when they say they will. The answer is "No." It's time to let go and do what you need to do for yourself.

A geriatrics assessment will let you know if your seniors are mentally capable. If they are not, call the local Adult Protective Services (APS) program or the Office of the Public Guardian (an attorney who works for the state and supervises guardianship petitions for persons whose assets exceed a level determined by each state).

If seniors are mentally capable, they have the right to make bad decisions. Some states have self-neglect laws, however, if a senior knows what he is doing and refuses help, there is no way to help.

Even if you believe that God always answers prayer, there comes a point when you must accept that, at least for the moment, the answer is "**NO**." Do what you can, make your referrals, and do what you need to do for yourself. Things may have to get worse before they can get better.

### You Did Your Best; Let God Do the Rest

After you've done what you can, give notice and step aside. Sometimes, other caregivers will step up. Sometimes, the only thing you can do is keep your eyes and ears open. Call to monitor the situation yourself or enlist the aid of others (family, neighbors, or social service agencies). When the person is ready to accept help, if you can assist, you can step back in. Even if you can't be hands-on when they call, you can always give empathy and information. Either way, conserve your energy and take care of yourself.

### Be Resilient; Roll with It

Resilience is the ability to take a punch and get back up instead of being shattered in the face of trouble. Dr. Cynthia T. Henderson was the first person from whom I heard, "Blessed are the flexible, for they shall not be bent out of shape." Resilience also generates peace in the face of chaos. Don't be so rigid that your plan completely breaks down after an obstacle. Always have a Plan B (sometimes C and D, too). I ask caregivers to consider, "What would I do if…?" and plan accordingly.

Get advice and help to look at the problem from another angle. Caregiver support groups are a great resource. Other caregivers may have already encountered your challenge and managed in a way you hadn't considered. Even if no one has dealt with your specific problem, someone may see it with a fresh eye and come up with a new solution. Resilience is more useful than panic, resentment, despair, or anger.

### The Angry Caregiver

Caregiving can generate serious anger, especially when you believe the person you care for has not treated you well.

# They Didn't Take Good Care of You<sub>(27)</sub>

*****************************

Ella McLeod brought her mother to the geriatrics center because of memory loss. Mrs. McLeod was a robust, stern seventy-eight-year-old who had been confined to a wheelchair for more than ten years because diabetes had damaged the nerves in her legs. Ella had also supervised the care of her father until he died from Parkinson's disease two years earlier.

The geriatrics team noted that Ella was quiet. They also thought she was nervous. She was in constant motion and seemed to anticipate her mother's need for tissues, water, and snacks. She continually asked if her mother was comfortable and changed Mrs. McLeod's position in the wheelchair frequently. Ella said very little in her mother's presence, yet when the team interviewed her alone, she demonstrated that she was a knowledgeable and capable caregiver. Ella admitted to being stressed and expressed no hope that anything could change. She reported that she was an only child and her parents had been strict and disparaging of her looks, her intelligence, her career aspirations, and her desirability to men and friends. Ella had never married and had few social contacts. She said, "They said I was here to take care of them. That's just the way it is."

At the end of the first office visit, the geriatric nurse practitioner accompanied both women to the parking lot to help Ella get her mother into the car. The nurse asked a question and when the women answered simultaneously, Mrs. McLeod screamed, "Don't interrupt." She backhanded her daughter and sent her sprawling onto the pavement.

Ella was even quieter in the follow-up visit and this time refused a separate interview. The geriatrics team thought she looked tired and stressed.

Mrs. McLeod refused adult day and respite services as well as the in-home help the team recommended. She laughed when the social worker recommended counseling, and Ella said nothing. Mrs. McLeod refused when the team wanted to arrange for a social worker from the community Department on Aging to visit the home. Ella still said nothing. The professionals worried that it was only a matter of time before something terrible happened. Unfortunately, since both parties were capable of decision-making, the team could do nothing.

Several months later, Ella was so tired that she went to bed without cleaning the kitchen. She had felt awful for several weeks. She hadn't been able to eat much, and her stomach was always queasy despite the antacid tablets she chewed all day.

The next morning, Mrs. McLeod screamed at her daughter about the dirty dishes. Instead of rushing to wash them as she would have in the past, Ella just sat at the kitchen table. She did not have the energy to move. When Mrs. McLeod rolled up to Ella and raised her hand this time, Ella twisted her mother's wrist hard enough to leave a bruise. As Mrs. McLeod yelped in pain, Ella doubled over and collapsed to the floor.

The ambulance took Ella to the hospital, where doctors diagnosed a bleeding ulcer that required a blood transfusion. No one was available to take care of Mrs. McLeod so social service workers arranged for her to move into an assisted-living community for the disabled. She agreed, saying, "It's just until the girl gets better."

Mrs. McLeod stayed in assisted-living because Ella decided to travel with the missionary ministry at her church. She also joined the choir and enrolled in a skills-training program through the church's employment ministry. She got a job as a receptionist for a local realtor. She visits Mrs. McLeod for dinner twice a week, and continues to work with a behavioral health counselor.

*************************

In *Drama of the Gifted Child*,[28] Dr. Alice Miller tells us that parents or other loving adults are supposed to fill a child's "unconditional love" tanks by a specific time in the child's development. When parents are inadequate or abusive, that special time passes, and the childhood love tanks never fill. Even though there are adult love tanks to fill, Dr. Miller says many adults keep trying to fill the childhood tanks. This may involve continued expectations of the parent or seeking similar satisfaction from other people. This causes painful problems for their relationships, careers, and overall happiness. This can be especially difficult for caregivers.

According to Dr. Miller, the effects of unhealthy parenting can either stop or continue to the next generation. I believe the impact can also go backwards and increase the risk of elder abuse and neglect. If a previously abused child/caregiver identifies with the parent in the abusive relationship, the caregiver is more likely to remember that she was defenseless and unable to protect herself as a child. This caregiver may think, "Now, I'm in control; I won't let him hurt me ever again." If a caregiver identifies with the abused child, he also recalls the hurt but says, "Now, I'm in control; I'll make sure no one ever feels the way I felt." According to Dr. Miller, even though they were hurt as children, if as adults, people can identify with the injured child, they are emotionally healthier and can stop the "cycle of contempt."

Get counseling to manage your anger and balance healthy caregiving with self-care. That is what our caregiver, Ella, did. Instead of allowing the situation to poison her spirit or damage her health any further, she learned how to see to her mother's care and create joy for herself.

## If Parents Knew Better, They'd Do Better

I do not believe most parents intend to hurt their children. Unlike driving, getting married, careers, and other adult responsibilities, parenting does not require pre-screening, training, or a license. Neither do kids come with an operator's manual. For good or ill, we learn how to parent by being around people who are parents. Many of us had negative relationships with our mothers and fathers. Though I do not excuse abusive or neglectful parents, I agree with my grandmother who said, "People can't give you what they don't have."

## You've Had You Longer Than Your Parents Had You

Many caregivers blame their unhappiness and failure in careers, finances, or relationships on the fact that their parents treated them badly. Isn't it time to work through the blame, accept responsibility for changing your life, and move forward?

✴✴✴✴✴✴✴✴✴✴✴✴✴✴✴✴✴✴✴✴✴✴✴✴

Mrs. Barrington had been a powerful, demanding, and distant mother. She was proud that both her daughters had earned master's degrees. Her younger daughter, Fay, was forty-seven years old and lived several hundred miles away. The older one, Ann, age fifty-three, lived in the same town. Although Ann had been estranged from her mother for several years, when she lost her job, she moved back into her mother's home.

This situation had lasted about a year when neighbors called the older daughter to report Mrs. Barrington's erratic driving. They got no response from Ann so, they contacted Fay. Even though she lived out of state, Fay arranged a geriatrics assessment and convinced her sister to provide transportation.

After the evaluation, I scheduled a family conference. Ann repeatedly interrupted her mother. "You won't do anything I tell you," she screamed. "And you never ever listened to me. You always put me down; that's why I can't find a job. I'm too nervous after all these years of dealing with you."

Mrs. Barrington gave as good as she got. She replied, "Ann, you have always been nuts."

In a separate interview, Mrs. Barrington denied feeling unsafe. In fact, she raised her fist in the air and said, "She better not mess with me." Mrs. Barrington also said she hated being around her older daughter because "She always keeps up some kinda mess."

Fay attended the family conference by phone while Mrs. Barrington and Ann were in the office. As the conference facilitator, I had to stop Ann's screaming several times. I also had to point out that this behavior worsened her mother's agitation. Part of the recommended care plan included a change in the caregiving situation.

Fay arranged for her sister to move in with another relative and hired a full-time companion and driver for her mom. I referred Ann to a community health clinic and behavioral health service for the uninsured. I also recommended a local workforce development center for employment counseling.

★★★★★★★★★★★★★★★★★★★★★★★★★

By the time most people become caregivers, they are well past legal age. If your parent's responsibility stopped when you were eighteen years of age and you are older than thirty-six, you've had yourself longer than your parents had you. If your life is not all you want it to be, is it still their fault? Adults are responsible to seek professional help to overcome the impact of unhealthy parenting, work through memories that cause emotional turmoil, and manage continuing relationship stress. As I have said, a large part of being successful in this is to accept that you are an adult.

### Listen to Your Parents with "Big Kid Ears"

You're not eight years old, anymore; you *are* an adult. You *are* responsible for your own choices, and you do not *need* their approval. You really don't.

*If there's no threat, there's no fight.* Once you understand that you have total control of yourself in a situation, you can learn to feel less vulnerable, and the need to react with defensive anger will fade. You will come to understand that you can afford to let comments roll off your back and meet your senior's anger with patience. Believe me; I know this is easier said than done. Behavioral health counselors will help you work through your fear, hurt, and anger. Counselors can guide you to better communication and coping strategies. They can also help you accept that your seniors are who they are. You cannot prove your worth to them. They have to value you and give approval freely. Perhaps, they can't. Counselors can help you grieve that reality and move on to a healthier approach to the relationship.

## The Angry Spouse

Sometimes, a caregiver is responsible for a spouse with whom she shared a long, unhappy marriage. The results can be dangerous.

\*\*\*\*\*\*\*\*\*\*\*\*\*\*\*\*\*\*\*\*\*\*\*\*\*\*\*\*\*

Mr. and Mrs. Quinn married fifty years ago when he was a thirty-year-old attorney and she, an eighteen-year-old high school graduate. Mr. Quinn had a brilliant career. Mrs. Quinn was the perfect homemaker, mother, and hostess until their four children grew up, and she yearned for a different life outside the home. Mr. Quinn had belittled his wife's intelligence throughout their marriage. He had also ridiculed her efforts to return to school, develop her interests, or find employment. Despite this, Mrs. Quinn turned her love of crafting into a successful shop where she gave lessons and sold crafting supplies. She became active in the chamber of commerce and was inducted into the local business hall of fame. Mr. Quinn was never supportive and once he retired from the law, he was vocal about resenting his wife's interests outside of their home.

Mr. Quinn suffered a stroke that left him confused and unsteady on his feet. Mrs. Quinn took excellent care of him. She never left him alone; she took him to her shop, to meetings, and on outings with friends. The Quinn children arranged for a geriatrics assessment when their father became sexually inappropriate with his wife in public.

The geriatrics team noticed that Mr. Quinn was loud and friendly, chuckling about "keeping the little woman in line." Mrs. Quinn was quiet and smiled sweetly as she allowed her husband and children to do the talking.

During the physical examination, the geriatrician found that Mr. Quinn had strange bruise. Mrs. Quinn explained that her husband had fallen. However, the team thought it unlikely that he could have fallen in such a way that a long, linear bruise slashed diagonally across his chest.

When the team confronted Mrs. Quinn about the discrepancy, she broke down in tears. She admitted that her husband had been psychologically and physically abusive throughout their marriage and had frequently assaulted her with his sexual demands. She had made plans to divorce him until he suffered the stroke. She felt she could not leave.

Although Mrs. Quinn was committed to giving care, she had little time for herself; she was overwhelmed by her husband's sexual demands and by memories of a lifetime of abuse. This time, when he accosted her, she snatched his cane and struck out as she had never done in the previous fifty years.

The APS investigator found that Mrs. Quinn had acted in self-defense. Since Mr. Quinn had suffered no major injury and there was no evidence of past injuries, they closed the case and assessed that with support, future abuse was unlikely. The children agreed to support any course of action their mother chose, and she decided to continue caregiving. She worked with the geriatrics team to keep his health issues in control. The team arranged counseling for Mrs. Quinn to help her release years of repressed anger. They also arranged daily adult day services to engage Mr. Quinn and provide respite for Mrs. Quinn. The adult day activities left Mr. Quinn so tired in the evening that there were few outbursts at night. With respite services, Mrs. Quinn took regular vacations. The situation remained stable until Mr. Quinn had a second stroke, went into a nursing home, and died two years later.

✳✳✳✳✳✳✳✳✳✳✳✳✳✳✳✳✳✳✳✳✳✳✳✳✳

### The Results of Abuse

Past abuse can put caregivers and seniors at risk, whether the caregiver experienced this abuse as a child or as an adult.

Caregivers can:

- Live in fear, relive the past, and experience current abuse from the senior (like Ella McLeod and Mrs. Quinn).

- Wear themselves out as they try to prove they are worthy of love and undeserving of contempt. (See Karla in *Chapter 11: Emotional Health - Don't Whine; Hum*).

- Work too hard because they worry that they could give too little care in subconscious revenge (possible motivation for Ella, Karla, and Mrs. Quinn).

- Become abusive, themselves whether anger and revenge are conscious or not (possible for all the above caregivers).

## That Ship Has Sailed

Mental or physical illness may move seniors beyond the reach of conversations that could decrease tensions or bring resolution. This leaves caregivers unable to find closure or make peace with older adults who have hurt them. Unresolved feelings of anger can make these caregivers mistreat those seniors, as well as their spouses, children, employees, students, and others who may be unable to defend themselves.

Though the people in your care may have hurt you when you were defenseless, hurting them (or others) cannot heal your emotional wounds; it can only continue the evil. Is that justice?

Nothing can poison the spirit as thoroughly, or as insidiously, as anger. The feeling may be subconscious, though echoes of the reasons for the anger may simmer under the surface. This can tinge caregivers' motivations with the need for revenge, or to justify their actions. Under these circumstances, maintaining a safe caregiving situation can be quite a challenge.

If you are an angry caregiver, get professional help to find closure within yourself. Grieve empty childhood love tanks, accept that they will not be filled, and move on. Fill adult love tanks today through healthy relationships and activities that do not involve your seniors.

If you cannot find a constructive way to deal with your anger, make other care arrangements. Get out of the caregiving situation for your senior's sake and your own.


## The Power of Forgiveness

*When Forgiveness Doesn't Make Sense* is a compelling book by Robert Jeffress.[29] The author says forgiveness is essential for emotional and spiritual health though it has nothing to do with the people who hurt or disappointed you. Forgiveness means you *decide* that the person (or situation) has no further power to hurt you, and you are not going to suffer from it anymore. Dr. Jeffress says through prayer (and I believe also through counseling), you learn to change how you respond. It's like pulling the knife out of your heart.

When you don't forgive, you keep hurting and building resentment that can change the way you behave in other situations and relationships. "Unforgiveness" can destroy you and your family.

*************************

After one of my presentations, a man who introduced himself as Bryan asked for advice about a brother who would not help his five siblings care for their frail parents. Bryan said the situation had caused a rift in the family that led to arguments at family gatherings.

I asked what kind of scene his brother made at holiday gatherings, and Bryan said, "Oh, he'd better not make a scene. My sisters, brothers, and I don't even give him a chance. We don't invite him and his family. Others in the family think he should be there, and that's what causes the trouble." Bryan seemed to puff up as if he was proud of himself. "We're doing all the work, and we don't think he deserves to come. At holidays, he drops off food, presents, and leaves."

When I asked whether his brother was willing to contribute money, cut grass, buy groceries, or participate in ways other than direct care, Bryan waved that idea away. "We didn't ask him any of that," he said. "All of us take a shift at the house; he should do it, too. We can't let him think it's okay for him to shirk his responsibilities."

The situation had lasted more than four years.

✳✳✳✳✳✳✳✳✳✳✳✳✳✳✳✳✳✳✳✳✳✳✳✳✳

Although the siblings thought it was unfair that their brother refused direct care responsibilities, they did not see that they were unfair to him in return. He might have done something if they had *asked* him what he *could* do instead of *telling* him what he *had* to do. We can all understand why the siblings would be upset that their brother didn't help, but he is an adult. They had no right to punish him like a child. It didn't work anyway.

Four years of punishment had not changed their brother's behavior, though it changed their parents' legacy: the happy family they had intended to create. I pointed this out to Bryan and recommended that this family forgive.

The first step in forgiveness is to stop judging. You don't know why some family members won't help. Maybe they can't. Maybe the person who was such a good mother to you wasn't such a good mother to your sister. It's possible that your grandfather was so wonderful that your brother can't bear to see him ill.

You can never know the true status of a relationship that doesn't involve you. It doesn't matter what actually happened in a situation. What matters is what people *believe* happened and how they *feel*. That's what motivates their behavior. Even if you think you know the facts, you cannot dispute their feelings.

Neither can you decide what other people owe your senior. You can't spend other people's time or their money. You can't fully understand their other responsibilities or order their priorities. Even if you could, you have no right to try to control their behavior.

How would you react if other family members told you what to do with or for your senior? How would you respond if they said you should spend *less* time giving care? Would their opinions change your behavior? Do you understand why your comments have no impact on the behavior of others?

Dr. Jeffress says forgiveness doesn't mean it's okay for people to hurt or disappoint you. Forgiveness does not require that offenders change their behavior. They do not have to be sorry or even know they need pardon. Neither does forgiveness mean that you must pretend hurtful actions aren't happening, let them continue, or maintain the same relationship. If you can't remove yourself from the interaction, you can get help to move your feelings and protect yourself emotionally. Like Bryan and his family, you can also stop doing what you're doing to escalate the situation (it's not working, anyway, is it?). Can you:

- Ask for the help you need and find out what people can and *will* do? (*See Chapter 8: Get Help from Family and Friends - "Ye Have Not Because Ye Ask Not"*)

- Stop judging and stop trying to punish people who aren't doing what you want?

- Stop relying on the unreliable by continuing to expect action from people who don't act? (*See Chapter 11, Protect Your Emotional Health - Avoid Disappointment -Don't Lean on Reeds*)

- Accept that you can't control others' behavior?

- Stop worrying about who *should* do something, get help from people who *want* to help, or hire help? (*See Chapter 8: Get Help from Family and Friends - "There's no SHOULD, there's only IS"*)

To paraphrase Dr. Jeffress, some people won't forgive because they enjoy the attention they get from broadcasting their martyrdom. Others enjoy feeling superior to the other person. Is this you? Don't you have something better to do?

"Unforgiveness" destroys YOU. Put aside pride, anger, and other negative emotions that flow between you and other family members. (In this game of "chicken," the person who is more spiritually mature is the one who blinks.) A counselor can help you deal with these feelings.

It isn't necessary to pretend that what happened (or what did not happen) was right. Forgiveness means that is irrelevant. Feeling and acting hurt or angry doesn't change the amount of work you're doing; it just intensifies your pain. Through forgiveness, you can free yourself from that pain and continue to give excellent care with less stress. Forgiveness allows you to stop wasting yourself on negativity and retain every ounce of your power to pull together a team, take care of your senior, and yourself.

### ALL Caregiving is Difficult; ALL Caregivers Deserve Support

Some caregivers believe they should not feel stress because they do not support several seniors, change dressings, do heavy lifting, or manage complicated medicine schedules. Even though these caregivers don't think they deserve respite and other support as much as others, they do.

Regardless of your level of responsibility, respect *your* needs. Remember it's self-*care* not self*ish*. Get the support you need to give excellent eldercare without endangering your senior's primary resource. *YOU!*

It is important to protect your physical, financial, emotional, and spiritual health, but that's not all you have to protect.

# CHAPTER 13

# When Eldercare Puts Other Relationships at Risk

Caregiving can consume so much energy that you have no time for other relationships. Everyone involved can suffer as you decide how to juggle your commitments.

### Forsaking All Others: *Your Marriage and Family*

Some caregivers focus solely on caregiving and become blind to the needs of their spouses and children.

\* \* \* \* \* \* \* \* \* \* \* \* \* \* \* \* \* \* \* \* \* \* \* \* \* \*

Mr. Thompson's mother became bedridden after a stroke. He refused nursing home care and community services because he didn't want strangers to care for her. He insisted that his wife quit her job and become his mother's caregiver, and his wife agreed. The next year his wife developed lupus (an autoimmune illness that left her tired and in pain). Although she was no longer able to handle things alone, Mr. Thompson still refused help.

He insisted that their two teenagers give up their activities to help after school and on weekends. The kids became increasingly sullen, and their school performance suffered.

Fatigue, pain, stress, resentment, and the lack of "couple time" undermined the communication and intimacy in the Thompson marriage. When his wife announced her intent to file for divorce and move to her sister's home with the children, Mr. Thompson realized he did not want to lose his family.

He called the local Department on Aging and found that his mother was eligible for caregiver service four hours every weekday. His mother's funds helped support hired caregivers for some of the other weekday hours as well as week of respite care twice a year. He asked church members to help for a few hours every other weekend. His wife and kids still pitched in by rotating responsibilities with the other caregivers. Everyone has time for themselves, their activities, and each other.

*************************

In his book, *Marriage on the Rock: God's Design for Your Dream Marriage*, Pastor Jimmy Evans says that our first family allegiance is to our spouse.[30] This can be a stressful choice because of the love and respect we have for our parents. I have seen many marriages fail under the strain of caregiving. Couples need to anticipate this challenge, factor it into caregiving decisions, and enlist the proper support to avoid risking their marriages.

### Painful Choice: The Generation that Created You versus The Generation You Are Creating: *Your Children*

When eldercare conflicts with childcare, caregivers face an agonizing choice.

*************************

My daughter was about eighteen months old when my mother (who had dementia) first came to live with us. One day, my baby went into the hospital with a stomach virus that caused massive diarrhea and dehydration. Her father and I made a commitment that our daughter would never wake up without seeing a familiar face. Our friends took shifts with us to make this possible.

One Sunday, my husband had to work and none of our friends were available to either be at the hospital with my daughter or at home with my mother. We had learned it was not safe to leave Mother alone when she placed a dish towel on the stovetop. The smoke detector had screeched while our five-year-old son ran to get the fire extinguisher and yelled a warning to his dad and me. Through all the noise, Mother just stood there. She stared at the flames in calm confusion, saying, "Why is this happening? This never happened before."

If Mother had been at home alone, she could have died. If she had been alone with my children, we could have lost all three of them (my son would have lost time trying to convince Grandmom to move. I doubt that he could have rescued the baby).

I had no other choice than to take Mother to the hospital with me. We had been there only a short time when she insisted on going outside to smoke. At this point in her dementia, Mother was very friendly; she greeted everyone like a long-lost friend and offered money to everyone who responded. Even so, she could no longer communicate well enough to get assistance if she got lost or had an emergency. The hospital was in a major urban area with all the dangers of an inner-city location. I did not want to leave my baby, but if I let Mother go out alone, she might be involved in a mugging or worse!

The baby was sleeping. There were several nurses on the floor and the sides of the hospital crib were high enough that she could not climb out and fall. My daughter might wake while I was gone and even if she was frightened, I knew she would be safe.

I agonized over the decision and finally, I left my baby with the nurses and went out with my mother. The next week, I sent Mother back to our hometown where there were more available family caregivers. We also hired helpers and asked people from Mother's church to fill any gaps in the care schedule.

I never wanted to have to choose between my mother and my children, ever again.

✳✳✳✳✳✳✳✳✳✳✳✳✳✳✳✳✳✳✳✳✳✳✳✳✳

Mrs. Johnson brought her mother, Mrs. Ingalls, to live with her when the senior could no longer live alone. Mrs. Johnson's seven-year-old son had a learning challenge with high-energy behaviors. Mrs. Ingalls would become agitated and follow him around the house, yelling. The boy's teachers reported that he was much more distracted and his behavior had become more disruptive since his grandmother joined the household. Mrs. Johnson punished the boy by taking away TV privileges and playtime with his friends. Still, his grades and behavior continued to decline. One day, Mrs. Johnson found her son hiding in the basement sobbing, "Mommy, I asked her to leave me alone; she just won't leave me alone."

Mrs. Johnson moved her mother into an assisted-living community. She visits several times each week—sometimes with her son, sometimes alone. She also brings Mrs. Ingalls home for a weekend every month and often arranges a sleepover for her son at the same time. His behavior and school performance have improved. Everyone feels less stressed.

* * * * * * * * * * * * * * * * * * * * * * * *

Caregivers have such pain when the needs of seniors and children conflict. It was our parents' job to prepare us for adulthood. They deserve respect and gratitude for helping us become the people we are today. It is our job to prepare our children to become successful citizens, employees, spouses, and parents who can influence future generations. In the chapter "On Children" in his classic book, *The Prophet,* Kahlil Gibran helps us put these allegiances into perspective. To paraphrase, he says that time circles forward, not backward; the parent's role is to serve as the bow in the Creator's hands so the arrows (children) can fly far and straight.[31]

Medical science cannot yet cure dementia, diabetes, advanced cancers, severe diseases of the heart, liver, and lung, or other chronic conditions that limit your senior's time on this planet. However, the environment in which children grow and the stressors in that environment have significant impact on their futures. If you must choose, *choose the children.*

## Until Death Do Us Part - *Don't Sacrifice The Healthy Parent*

Caregivers can be so focused on the sick parent that they neglect the other one and risk losing them both.

* * * * * * * * * * * * * * * * * * * * * * * *

Dr. Seals had been a prominent surgeon and politician in his community. When he developed a debilitating illness and became increasingly frail, his children still refused to let anyone know he was ill.

After a year, Mrs. Seals started to lose her battle with caregiving responsibility. She was short of breath, tired, and tearful. The family did not want to erode Dr. Seals' political influence, tarnish his reputation, or "ruin his legacy" so they refused all caregiving help. One day, Mrs. Seals noticed a strange ache in her shoulders and jaw. She shrugged it off, took two aspirin, and prepared lunch for Dr. Seals and a visiting colleague. Suddenly, the pain intensified and Mrs. Seals could not catch her breath. She was lucky that Dr. Seals' friend called 9-1-1. Mrs. Seals had suffered a mild heart attack. When the family realized how close they came to losing Mom too, they hired help.

\*\*\*\*\*\*\*\*\*\*\*\*\*\*\*\*\*\*\*\*\*\*\*\*

It can be quite a challenge to balance the needs of sick elders and healthy ones. There is no way to know how many good years are ahead for a healthy senior. Instead of penalizing her or being the last one standing, help her live her remaining time to the fullest. Make his caregiving as easy as possible, and see that his life is about more than caregiving. Make sure she gets to do the things she loves, whether it's attending a religious service or a poker game, going to a book club meeting, or traveling with friends.

You cannot change the dependent senior's disability or their future; the healthy seniors still have many opportunities to enjoy life. *Do not sacrifice the people who have good time left and...*

## Don't Sacrifice Their Relationship

When a healthy senior's spouse lives in a care facility, the separation can threaten their identity as a couple.

\*\*\*\*\*\*\*\*\*\*\*\*\*\*\*\*\*\*\*\*\*\*\*\*

Mr. and Mrs. McNabb had been together for seventy years. He was eighty-seven years old; she was eighty-five and they had been a couple since high school.

Mr. McNabb fell, broke his hip, and never regained enough mobility to return to his home. The family chose an excellent care facility within blocks of the McNabb's house. Facility administrators allowed family members to share occasional meals at low cost but were not sensitive about maintaining the McNabb's relationship. Mr. McNabb had a roommate and nursing home policy did not allow the couple any privacy. The husband and wife missed each other so much that the health and function of both seniors began to decline.

\*\*\*\*\*\*\*\*\*\*\*\*\*\*\*\*\*\*\*\*\*\*\*\*

Families and care facilities should recognize that separation after decades of marriage may be especially painful for couples. Facilities should offer opportunities for residents to remain a couple, including conjugal time, if they both wish it. A recent controversy questioned whether a nursing home resident with dementia could consent to sexual activity with her healthy husband. Aside from this difficult situation, when decision-making capacity is not an issue, nursing home administrators should plan for consenting couples to enjoy privacy and intimacy. This may be a challenge with two-resident rooms, but if prisons can arrange special areas for conjugal visits, why can't nursing homes do the same?

As you investigate potential care facilities, ask questions about opportunities for couples to participate in activities together and enjoy private time.

### Your Life: *"My Senior DEMANDS All My Time"*

The love, respect, and gratitude we feel towards our parents can make it difficult to draw the necessary boundaries to live our own lives.

*************************

Ms. Black had cared for her mother, Mrs. Unger, for most of her adult life. Although Ms. Black fell in love and became engaged, she put off marriage, postponed buying a home, and waived other life passages. She was reluctant to take vacations with her fiancé because her mother "got sick" whenever Ms. Black did not focus full attention on her.

Ms. Black worried that life was passing her by and became stressed and depressed. Eventually, she was unable to leave her home. Through supportive psychotherapy, she realized that she deserved an independent life. She also realized her mom was being unreasonable.

Ms. Black arranged for her mother to attend an adult day program where the caregivers doted on her. Ms. Black got married and her mother came to love her son-in-law because he doted on her too. Eventually, the couple moved with the senior into a home with an attached, private suite and used a baby monitor to check on Mrs. Unger at night. Whenever the couple took a vacation or went out for the evening, they hired one of the caregivers from the adult day center privately. Though Mrs. Unger grumbled, she was okay.

*************************

## *You Owe Your Parents Your Existence, Not Your Life*

Parents and adult children can experience clashing needs and expectations. While parents deserve to be treated with love, respect, comfort, and reasonable consideration, they are not entitled to all your time, energy, or resources. Never are they entitled at the expense of your marriage, family, and joy.

When there is a health crisis or if the elder is near death, of course, everyone will adjust and focus on the senior for a time. However, other important relationships and priorities should never be in permanent danger.

Your marriage, your children, the healthy parent, and YOU have futures that can change and improve; investments in these futures can have significant, long-term, positive effects. For frail seniors, the future is more limited. Respect your senior's priorities and relationships as you attend to their health and comfort. However, if you must choose, invest in the future, those who have good time left, and those whose remaining time can have lasting impact on others.

In this section you learned about the cost of caregiving to your physical, financial, emotional, and spiritual health. I know how hard it is to think about your own needs and recognize that self-**care** is not sel**fish**. Please remember to ask yourself these questions:

- Why do I protect my elder's health, home, finances, and happiness yet forget to care for the *single resource* that makes *everything* possible? Why don't I protect my senior's *caregiver?*

- I am willing to give until it hurts. Why must I give until I am *damaged?* Why must I sacrifice *my* health, finances, relationships?

You can't be a good caregiver if you're sick, impoverished, depressed, isolated, eaten by anger and non-forgiveness, soul-weary, or no longer alive. As we take care of everyone else, let's try to feel okay about taking care of ourselves too.

It is hard to feel okay when the caregiving process can cause so much pain. The next section offers specific skills and support to help you get through.

# How Do You Manage When Your Heart Is Bleeding?

Caregiving can cause pain as we grieve the changes that illness causes in our seniors and in our relationships with them (living grief). We also fear the changes that may come next (anticipatory grief). Pain also comes from the weight of having to make very tough decisions. Decisions toward the end of the caregiving season can make these feelings more intense especially when we cannot:

- Acknowledge the effects of different types of grief.

- Commit to and be persistent in having compassionate conversations with our seniors, and listen to what they believe makes life worth living.

- Encourage them to prepare documents that make those values clear.

- Continue to give excellent care and advocate for our loved ones with informed and compassionate decisions even when those decisions are difficult.

- Forgive ourselves when we have to make the best possible choice from equally sad options.

# CHAPTER 14

# The Weight of Grief

**"Living Grief" Begins Long Before Your Loved One Passes On**

Long before seniors die, they grieve the loss of their independence, and you grieve it for them. You also grieve changes in your relationship. I call this "living grief."

\* \* \* \* \* \* \* \* \* \* \* \* \* \* \* \* \* \* \* \* \* \* \* \* \*

Mr. and Mrs. McDonald enjoyed a circle of friends with whom they had gone bowling, played cards, and enjoyed plays, movies, and restaurants in their fifty-five years of marriage. Mrs. McDonald suffered a series of strokes and at first, the group tried to involve her in their usual activities. However, with each stroke, she became less able to participate. She could not follow the strategy of card games or remember how to compute bowling scores. She forgot her friends' names, seemed puzzled by the simplest questions, and spent many evenings staring off into space.

When Mrs. McDonald began to lose control of her bladder, the friends found reasons to exclude her from their outings. They continued to invite

Mr. McDonald who refused to join them if he could not bring his wife. He was upset with his friends because they no longer wanted to interact with Mrs. McDonald. He told them so at every opportunity, and the friends stopped inviting him too. Eventually, the calls and visits stopped as well.

Mrs. McDonald's condition declined until she did not recognize her husband. Her withdrawal left him sullen and tearful; his friends' withdrawal left him angry and isolated.

*************************

Part of Mr. McDonald's anger was due to grief. He grieved his wife's illness and the loss of their friends' companionship. Mr. McDonald's grief was more for his wife than for himself because he thought she deserved better after such long friendships. He did not understand that his friends were grieving, too. They all suffered *living grief* as they watched Mrs. McDonald fade away. They did not know how to handle her illness nor how to deal with losing a part of their world. The friends were also probably a little frightened for her future and their own. I call this *anticipatory grief*: grieving for losses, yet to come.

Most seniors and their families experience both living and anticipatory grief. Grandpa's arthritis is so bad that he can't work on the cars he loves. How will he cope with losing his hobby? What will he lose next? Grandma's heart is so weak that she spends less time in her garden. What will make her happy if she gets to the point where she can't garden at all? How will she spend her days?

Living grief, anticipatory grief, and grieving the loss of relationship is especially painful when the illness is dementia.

### Grieving Dementia: the *"Slow Walk Home"* —Bishop T. D. Jakes

Bishop T.D. Jakes was right when he called dementia the "slow walk home."(32) A loved one's journey with dementia can last over twenty years.

*************************

I watched my mother die of dementia for ten years. I was married. I had children, an extended family, a church family, and a large support base of friends and colleagues. I was an experienced geriatrician and a woman of faith. Even so, I felt overwhelming pain as I watched dementia take another piece of my mother from me every day.

Long before her doctors gave the official diagnosis, I suspected that what ailed my mother was dementia. My physician-mind imagined each step of her decline in excruciating, clinical detail. This was anticipatory grief.

I also suffered ten years of living grief. Although Mother's body was here, our relationship was not. I had so many questions about my kids. Is it normal for my daughter to be doing this at her age? What should I do when my son does that? I wanted my mommy and although I could see, hear, and touch her, she was already gone.

In the last hours of Mother's life, I knelt at her bedside, held her hand to my face, and said, "Please don't leave me alone here." I knew I had lost Mother years before; I understood that it was best for Mother to move on and I thought I was prepared for her death. I was not at all prepared to feel abandoned. I was an experienced geriatrician and medical school faculty member; I had advocated for Mother in the healthcare system and had made the hard decisions. Still, in those last moments, I felt like a toddler whose mommy had left her alone in a huge shopping mall. I was just a frightened, grieving child.

*************************

When people suffer physical illness, their caregivers can see the weakness, weight loss, swelling, skin changes, and signs of pain. They can hear the sounds and smell the odors of illness. These factors remind caregivers that the loved one is in battle with a debilitating condition. Many people who have dementia remain physically healthy until late in the illness. They look like themselves and this allows caregivers to ignore or forget that changes are occurring. Family members' emotions continue to reach for a response that the senior will never give again. Families feel this pain every...single... time—every time they come into the house, every time they come into the room, every time they turn around.

Remember, there is no role reversal in caregiving (*See Chapter 7: Work with Your Senior, Watch Your Tone of Voice*). Even if your seniors have been dependent for years, they are still your seniors. As they decline, you miss their wisdom, humor, advice, and love. When they are sick or injured and when they die, you grieve like a child.

## A Grieving Spouse

While many adult children are in the double bind of having to be in control while they lose their parents' support, a grieving spouse suffers most of all.

\*\*\*\*\*\*\*\*\*\*\*\*\*\*\*\*\*\*\*\*\*\*\*\*\*\*\*\*

Remember Mr. and Mrs. McDonald from the beginning of this chapter. They had been high school sweethearts and were each the other's soul mate. Living grief devastated Mr. McDonald as he watched his wife slip away.

He became isolated when their friends withdrew, but he might have felt uncomfortable even if they had kept calling. Mr. McDonald had become a single in a couples' world. Though his wife's participation was painful for everyone, he might have felt awkward attending group functions by himself.

Mr. McDonald stopped going out and as a result, he spent more time alone with Mrs. McDonald. This intensified his loss. She could not recall their inside jokes, nor the ups and downs they had weathered together in fifty-five years of marriage. Not only had she forgotten their history, she no longer reacted to the sweet, intimate gestures they had shared. As the disease progressed, she did not even recognize her husband. One minute she was agitated because she thought he was a stranger who had come to hurt her. The next minute, she held on to him and sobbed. Mr. McDonald lost his soul mate, his life partner, and as the illness forced him to stand by and watch this happen, he lost the joy in his life.

\*\*\*\*\*\*\*\*\*\*\*\*\*\*\*\*\*\*\*\*\*\*\*\*\*\*\*\*

Even as adult children grieve their losses, they must have special consideration for the grieving spouse. Caregiving wives and husbands lose aspects of a relationship a child has never and could never have known. How can anyone else understand the countless little losses a spouse suffers, living with a partner who slowly shrinks away from more than fifty years of memories?

When you consider schedules, care locations, and other factors in caregiving, as much as possible, try to make it easier for the healthier spouse. As much as you hurt, their pain is so much worse.

### Grief and Guilt: *Wishing the Situation Would End*

When a person dies, happy memories can comfort us and make our grief easier to bear. When a person deteriorates before our eyes, reality gets between us and the memories, leaving no room for comfort. Living grief intensifies as we watch our loved one's physical suffering, growing dependence, and isolation in the illness. Anticipatory grief grows as you wonder what will happen next. Everyone grieves the loss of relationships. Why *wouldn't* you want it to be over for your seniors and for yourself?

Wishing the situation would pass does not mean you want the person dead so you can be free of caregiving. You just wish *everyone* could be free from the situation. Guilt about these feelings adds another layer of suffering as caregivers believe they are being selfish, heartless, or cruel. None of this is true. This just another aspect of their grieving.

Whether you grieve dementia or other chronic conditions, whether you grieve as a child, a spouse, or any other relative, whether the caregiving is physically demanding or not, the emotional toll from grief is *always* heavy. Talk to other caregivers, clergy, and eldercare consultants. Find a behavioral health specialist. Get the support you need to work through the grief and ease your pain. You deserve it.

One situation that burdens struggling caregivers with additional grief, guilt, and pain is the process of deciding whether your loved one should move into a nursing home.

# CHAPTER 15

## The Nursing Home Decision – When You Promised "Never!": Honor the SPIRIT of the Promise

Though many families think seniors get worse because they go into a nursing home, healthy people do not require twenty-four-hour nursing care. Therefore, by definition, nursing home residents are not healthy. Most nursing home residents have end-stage, chronic conditions that have progressed past the possibility of cure. Some of these seniors had received good care at home until they experienced a flare of their chronic conditions. Others had been doing okay with their chronic illness, but these diseases left them vulnerable to attack by new problems. Either way, their care needs increased beyond what either they or their caregivers could provide. Being at home was no longer safe.

Some new nursing home residents become depressed, grieve the loss of their homes and independence, lose the will to live, and decline quickly. Even so, the primary cause of the decline is the underlying illness, not the nursing home, per se. Should these seniors and their families have ignored the fact that the necessary care was no longer available at home? Should the seniors have risked more suffering by staying at home, when it was no longer safe?

Although a senior with memory loss may appear to get worse when he moves into a nursing home, his brain was just as damaged at home. He only seemed to function better in his own environment because in the decades when his brain was healthy, he encoded information about the layout of the house, placement of the furniture, schedules, and routines. Once the illness struck, the senior began to rely on these cues to cover the fact that he could no longer remember. When he goes into a nursing home, he moves away from these reminders and can no longer hide how serious his memory loss has become. (This can also happen when seniors move to or even visit a relative's home that should be familiar). The illness also makes it impossible for the senior to form new memories or even pull up the old ones fast enough to avoid accidents. Being at home is no longer safe.

If a senior dies shortly after moving into a nursing home, her family may regret their decision and feel that either they or the nursing home killed their loved one. While some nursing homes give poor care, in most cases, neither the family nor the facility caused the senior's death. Often, the problem is that the nursing home decision came too late. Families often refuse to consider a nursing facility until the seniors' illnesses are so advanced or the caregivers are so tired, sick, or injured that there is no way to provide good care at home. In fact, the quality of care may have been slipping for some time. When these seniors move into the nursing home, their health is poor, at best. Then, they do what their chronic illnesses dictate; they get worse, and they die.

When I was in practice, I tried to help families avoid these late decisions. Well before the need became obvious (often, as soon as I presented the LOCRx), I asked, *"What changes (in the senior, yourself, or the overall situation) would make you decide that you could no longer care for him at home?"*

My goal was to have the families draw a line. As our relationship continued and the illness progressed, I could remind the family of the boundaries they set. When the care needs increased and we approached that boundary, I would raise the nursing home issue, so the family did not have to.

As they answered my question, many caregivers realized their loved one's illness was already so advanced and the caregiver, already so overwhelmed that they had crossed the line months or even years before I asked.

Other caregivers used those boundaries to make proactive plans. Each time changes brought them closer to the "impossible point," these families recruited more resources and moved the line. They knew the nursing home would be the only alternative when they could no longer provide more resources. When the time came, they did not feel guilty because they knew they had done all they could.

Caregivers and seniors can have a better experience when they do not wait until the last minute to use the nursing home. When families allow the nursing home staff to handle day-to-day care, caregivers are free to do things *with* and *for* their loved ones, not *to* them. This makes the time they spend with the elder good time. It also frees caregivers to concentrate on advocating for their senior.

### Stay in Control of the Care Plan

Even though your senior is in the nursing home, you are still the caregiver. You do not give up the rights or the responsibility for your senior's care. You can serve their best interests only when you are a strong advocate. That means having an effective voice to raise your concerns. The first step is to get all necessary information from every possible source.

### It Takes a Village to Raise a Child AND to Support a Senior: *Make Other Families Your Allies*

Families of residents in long-term care facilities can join forces to watch out for everybody's loved ones.

\*\*\*\*\*\*\*\*\*\*\*\*\*\*\*\*\*\*\*\*\*\*\*\*\*\*

Mrs. Carter and Mrs. Nagle had been roommates in the nursing home for more than a year. Members of the Carter and Nagle families chatted when they ran into each other on visits and eventually got to know each other well.

When Mrs. Carter's daughter came to visit, she would see Mrs. Nagle playing bingo in the hall and get a full report about her mom. Mrs. Nagle would laugh and say, "Your mom's still tellin' jokes and runnin' things." Sometimes, Mrs. Nagle would look worried. "She's not feeling well today. She didn't eat all her lunch."

At one point, the nursing assistants commented that Mrs. Nagle seemed more irritable and less interested in playing bingo. They also informed the registered nurse (RN) that she had soiled her underpants and hidden them in the bathroom. The staff seemed to think Mrs. Nagle was "just getting worse."

A couple of weeks later, the nursing home administrator called Mrs. Carter's daughter to inform her that the facility planned to move her mother to another room. The administrator also said Mrs. Nagle had become verbally abusive to Mrs. Carter, and they decided to separate the ladies for safety reasons.

Mrs. Carter's daughter was concerned—about Mrs. Nagle. The change in behavior was not consistent with the long-standing relationship between the two roommates. Mrs. Carter's daughter contacted Mrs. Nagle's daughter.

Mrs. Nagle's family discussed the changes with the nurse who alerted the doctor. The diagnosis was a severe urinary tract infection. After a course of antibiotics and a few days in the hospital, Mrs. Nagle returned to the nursing home and her roommate.

\*\*\*\*\*\*\*\*\*\*\*\*\*\*\*\*\*\*\*\*\*\*\*\*\*\*\*

Get to know your loved one's roommate's family. Good relations can make the environment more pleasant for the seniors and offer mutually supportive relationships for caregivers. These alliances can also stretch caregiver resources as one family keeps an eye on things when the other family isn't there. This creates an early warning system. Changes in behavior can be the first signs of treatable illness. Roommates often see changes before the professionals do. They can alert staff and families before conditions deteriorate. Do not miss the opportunity to form teams with other families.

### Get to Know the Nursing Home Staff Too

This is not just a ploy; it is a way to develop relationships that contribute to a cooperative and pleasant situation for everyone. Security guards, receptionists, dietary, and housekeeping staff can offer useful information about the facility. Although you cannot expect these workers to be spies or informants, casual conversations can offer critical information about the culture and quality of life in the facility. This information can either ease your mind, let you know it is time to voice a concern, or guide your decision about making a change.

## Follow the Chain of Command

Families can become frustrated when they do not get the answers they need. Sometimes, this happens because they asked the wrong person.

The registered nurse (RN) on your senior's care unit should be your first point of contact about any concerns or complaints. The RN will also know about medicines, wound care, catheters, specific treatments, and changes in health.

Certified nursing assistants (CNAs) and the nursing aides who provide direct care are the best source of information about a resident's behavior. For example:

- How is Dad eating?

- Does he control his bowels and bladder?

- How does he react to bathing and other care?

- How well does he participate in activities and get along with other residents?

- Does he need any toiletries, clothing, or supplies?

You usually have casual conversations with CNAs when you visit your relative. You can ask for more formal discussions with them or with rehabilitation therapists, psychologists, and social workers but remember, speak with the RN first.

If the nursing staff cannot resolve your concerns or if there are serious or repeated problems, contact the director of nursing. If you are not satisfied with the director's input, make an appointment with the nursing home administrator.

The doctor should take questions about health issues and medicines. Nurses and other nursing home staff are not the most effective line of communication with doctors. (See *Chapter 6, The Physician User's Manual*) The most effective way to reach a doctor is through the doctor's private office. You can find contact information on the Internet if the nurses do not seem comfortable giving you the phone number.

## Attend the Quarterly Care Conferences

Nursing home regulations require the staff to review residents' care plans at least every three months. The social worker or care coordinator must notify the family of the conference time in advance. If you give enough notice and are flexible, you can reschedule the conference to a more convenient time.

Bring a list of questions and concerns to the meeting. You may also bring an advocate (another family member, clergy, or an eldercare consultant) and you may take notes. Ask about the facility's policy on recording the sessions. Also ask:

- How will the facility resolve any problems the team finds?
- Which staff members are responsible for each issue?
- How they will monitor the solutions?
- When should we expect an update?
- Who is our contact person?

In previous generations, nursing home residents did not have intravenous medicines, oxygen, or complicated treatment plans. Today, your senior's condition may be more complex and you may feel the need for a conference more often than every ninety days. Though is it unlikely that all the team members can accommodate more frequent conferences, you should be able to arrange a meeting with the RN, social worker, therapist, or the physician when you have a specific concern.

### Contact the Ombudsman

Most states assign an advocate to address accusations of mistreatment, safety issues, and other serious problems in the nursing home. Ombudsmen are not nursing home employees. They are independent volunteer investigators and mediators. Departments on aging educate them about how to work with nursing home administrators, residents, and families. The nursing home will have contact information for the ombudsman assigned to that facility. The Department on Aging or the Area Agency on Aging are independent sources for this information.

### BE NICE!

Even though you have every right to raise your concerns, it's better to start out by being nice. You can always "mean-up" later if need be, but it can be very difficult to recover from a bad first impression.

Be professional and courteous. *Always remember!* Sarcasm and condescension are just as bad as yelling and cursing. Though bad behavior makes people notice you, it overshadows and minimizes your concerns. If you want facility staff to take you seriously and respond appropriately, make sure they don't cringe when they see your name on the caller ID.

### Don't Just Be a Squeaky Wheel

No matter how nice you are, people will become insensitive to your needs if you only complain. Participate in holiday celebrations and special programs. Attend support groups and educational seminars. Bring your talents to the nursing facility (like you did for Parent-Teacher Association [PTA] programs when your children were in school). Most activities departments will gladly schedule your choirs, dancers, plays, movie discussions, crafts, and just about anything that can make residents smile.

Most facilities are also interested in staff development and educational programs for residents, families, and the community. Contact the activities director or social worker to schedule a topic of general interest. Contact the administrator if you have a specific skill or area of expertise and want to offer a program for the staff. Either way, prepare a brief description of the session, three ideas or pieces of information you want people to take away from the presentation (objectives,) and your credentials or experience.

### Give Yourself A Break if You Decide to Use a Nursing Home

I think of nursing homes as powerful treatments that can offer great benefits as well as negative side effects. Instead of making the promise that you will *never* use a nursing home, you and your family can honor the *spirit* of that promise: to *always give the best* care. There comes a time when giving the care yourself does not honor the promise. When families recognize their limitations and learn to be effective advocates, they avoid feeling guilty when being at home is no longer safe and a nursing home is the most appropriate care option.

Whether the care site is a nursing home, hospital, or the home, care decisions are especially challenging when seniors near their last days. Although decisions at the end of life are among the most stressful and guilt-producing of all caregiving responsibilities, it is possible to make these discussions less painful for everyone.

# CHAPTER 16

# End-of-Life Care:
# Adding Life to Years,
# Not Just Years to Life

M ost people never discuss their end-of-life wishes. This leaves their families to grapple with painful questions: "Are we doing the right thing? Would she have wanted this?" Families agonize and fight over these decisions. When they do not know what their loved one wanted, they also continue tests and treatments long past their usefulness.

Between 1947 (when penicillin became widely available) and 1984 (when the nation began to recognize the threat of Acquired Immune Deficiency Syndrome—AIDS or HIV), Americans lived in the era of *Cure*. In these years, medical science developed increasingly potent antibiotics and cancer chemotherapy. Doctors snatched people from the jaws of death with cardiopulmonary resuscitation (CPR), ventilators (breathing machines), and dialysis (to support failing kidneys). Science also developed the expertise to safely transplant almost every organ. Since the late 1990s, effective medicines have made HIV a chronic condition. We relaxed until 2019 when COVID-19 reminded us that medical science does not have control over death.

Even so, today's older adults, most of their caregivers, and most practicing healthcare professionals lived through these *Cure* years. We have come to expect medical miracles, and often focus on technology while failing to consider the outcome.

Our nation spends so much money on medical care, including drastic and sometimes abusive treatments that have no chance of curing terminal illnesses. We spend a lot of this money in the last weeks of life. Americans can avoid facing end-of-life decisions because medical science has allowed us to cling to three fallacies:

- Death is optional.

- Technology is God.

- Death is failure.

### Death is Not Optional

Between the era of the ancient pharaohs and 1947 (the release of penicillin), the world was in the age of **Care**; cure was rarely possible. Now the healthcare system may be headed backwards. The danger is not due to a lack of expertise or equipment. Medical professionals will still be able to perform dramatic surgeries and other treatments; they will not be able to cure the infections that follow. Bacterial infections have become increasingly resistant to common antibiotics. This problem and the emergence of Zika, the West Nile and Ebola viruses, Severe Acute Respiratory Syndrome (SARS,) Avian flu, COVID-19, and other serious viral infections threaten to put us back into that pre-Cure era. We will have to give up the illusion that death is optional.

### Technology is Not God

Dr. Bernie Siegel is a Yale cancer surgeon who wrote a series of moving books including *Love, Medicine and Miracles.*(33) He tells us that many people die quickly, even though their illnesses are supposed to respond to treatment. Others carry dismal diagnoses yet outlive their doctors. Science does not have all the answers.

We should embrace medical science when it can prevent illness, cure disease, or relieve suffering. However, machines and complicated treatments become irrelevant when they can neither offer comfort, nor change the conditions that cause death. No matter how exciting aggressive treatments appear, they are just treatments, with specific indications (reasons to use them) and contraindications (reasons not to use them). This requires conscious thought and very difficult decisions.

## Should We Do It Just Because We Can?

Doctors and families must not use technology just because it's there.

\*\*\*\*\*\*\*\*\*\*\*\*\*\*\*\*\*\*\*\*\*\*\*\*\*\*

Mrs. Conroy was an eighty-three-year-old woman with unexplained weight loss and anemia (low blood count). A common cause of these problems is a tumor in her bowels that causes slow, invisible bleeding over time. Mrs. Conroy also had a long history of high blood pressure, diabetes, and heart attacks that had severely damaged her heart. The doctors could administer only a slow and very small blood transfusion because her weakened heart could not tolerate the extra fluid.

Her family and doctors faced a decision. Should they perform a colonoscopy (passing a lighted tube through Mrs. Conroy's rectum and into her bowel) to see if she had a tumor? It is a relatively simple procedure to perform, though it can be uncomfortable. It was very likely that the anesthesia (medicine to block the pain) could make her confused. There was also a possibility of bleeding, infection, or perforation (poking a hole through the wall of the bowel) that could require emergency surgery.

Even if there were no complications, if doctors found a tumor, Mrs. Conroy's heart was too weak to survive surgery to remove it. If she did survive, she was at high risk of pneumonia, blood clots, infections, and permanent changes in memory and other brain functions. These conditions might leave her even more frail and could decrease her quality of life. After several discussion, Mrs. Conroy and her family decided it made no sense to perform the colonoscopy.

\*\*\*\*\*\*\*\*\*\*\*\*\*\*\*\*\*\*\*\*\*\*\*\*\*

Mrs. Conroy and her family considered the options and risks, and made a decision that the risks outweighed the benefits. At worst, the colonoscopy could cause harm; at best the procedure would find conditions for which the treatment might worsen her already poor health. Why impose even minimal discomfort or risk when the procedure will not provide information doctors can use to help the person? Why draw a map to a place we can't go? Another senior and family might have made a different decision. The key is not to jump into what is possible without considering what is best for a specific person.

I have often refused to authorize a test "just to know." When information will not cure, improve a condition, or ease suffering, I am perfectly willing to get the information at an autopsy, after the person has died and is beyond discomfort or risk.

Despite the worship of technology, the subspecialties of palliative care and hospice are growing. These programs support the belief that life is about more than a beating heart. As healthcare shifts focus to emphasize quality of life, I hope we come to accept that the real goal of medical treatment is not to just prolong life but to promote quality of life. When conditions are incurable, this goal includes a commitment to ease suffering.

Unfortunately, doctors are trained to cure. We often feel we have failed if we do not try everything to reach that goal. Many families also believe they have failed their loved one if they do not use every available treatment. This approach leads to avoidable suffering, unnecessary guilt, overuse of technology, and overwhelming healthcare costs.

**Death is Not Failure.**

*Why Do Some Doctors Think It Is?*

The explosion in medical science and the focus on cure has made technological "bells and whistles" seem more "doctorly" than words of comfort. Traditional medical education programs have promoted this belief by conducting most training in acute hospitals. They also seem to put less value on outcomes other than cure. Because of this, many doctors are unwilling to accept death as a natural part of life.

Also, most doctors have been A+ students since kindergarten. Many of us are internally driven, while for others, stellar grades resulted in pleased parents. People who need to bask in that pride and pleasure can develop approval addiction (see Joyce Meyer's book with the same title). Approval "addicts" feel threatened at a deep emotional level when they must face that no matter how hard we study or work, we can't always cure.

*Why Do Families Believe Death is Failure?*

Families are not immune to fears of failure that plague professionals. Some caregivers do not want to let their loved one down and insist on doing "everything." Unfortunately, their actions do not avoid the regret that comes when the person passes on. These families still torture themselves with the thought, "Maybe if I had done more, she wouldn't have died."

Some families overuse technology and keep loved ones alive not for the loved one but for themselves. Some people are emotionally dependent on the dying family member and cannot bear the thought of living without him. I do not think most families are aware of this motivation; they make subconscious decisions that prolong the loved one's dying (and suffering) so the surviving family members don't have to be alone.

Other families believe choosing to say "no" to inappropriate treatments at the end of life means "playing God by just letting people die." God does not need a ventilator. Neither does God need doctors to hold on to people until God gets back from lunch. Isn't it arrogant to presume that human science alone has the power to overcome death? When families insist on "doing everything" to stop people from dying, who's playing God?

Even if medical science can improve a condition for a time, death is the ultimate reality for everyone. (I have heard comedians say, "Nobody gets out of life alive.") Failure-avoidance makes families and healthcare professionals continue to use technology even when it does absolutely no good and even when it causes harm. This doesn't work for family or professional caregivers. It certainly doesn't work for the person for whom they give care.

## Why Are We Doing This?

When we use technology even though it cannot affect the illness, we often extend life long enough to allow worse problems to develop.

\*\*\*\*\*\*\*\*\*\*\*\*\*\*\*\*\*\*\*\*\*\*\*\*

Mrs. Carle had stopped eating because of end-stage Alzheimer's disease. Her caregiver wanted to talk about putting a feeding tube into her stomach.

As their doctor, I felt it was my responsibility to give the most complete information possible. I explained that while the tube would offer a way to give hydration (fluids) and nutrition (calories), it would not stop the illness. Mrs. Carle was dying from Alzheimer's, not dehydration or malnutrition. In this situation, a feeding tube would only make sure it took longer for her to die. In the extended time, their loved one would be at risk for pneumonia and other infections, pressure sores (bed sores), and blood clots. The tube would increase the length of living and the length of suffering.

Instead of making a snap decision, the caregiver decided to discuss this information with the extended family first. The family agreed on the hospice option without a tube.

We doctors pride ourselves on reviewing symptoms and other information to recommend the most beneficial treatment while avoiding unnecessary risk. Unfortunately, a lot of us forget this principle at the end of life. Some of the orders we write prolong suffering. In end-stage situations, maybe someone should write, *"Don't just do something! Stand there!"*

Doctors and families can be so intent on searching for the next possible treatment that they ignore that death *is* stalking the person. When dealing with advanced, chronic, incurable conditions, instead of looking down at each individual step, care teams should look ahead to see whether they are walking down the right road for the senior. The destination is the same; death is coming. When doctors and families push seniors down a road that will not improve their lives, those seniors pay the cost in suffering.

Hospice services provide compassionate care for the dying. Primary care doctors are in the best position to introduce families to hospice when we have long-term relationships with the people in our practices. We also know whether a condition (or the effect of several co-existing conditions) is terminal. I hope we also know the family well enough to understand their values.

### A Better Way

The term we use to decline the burden of useless machines, medicines, and other aggressive treatments may be a barrier to humane care at the end-of-life. Do Not Resuscitate (DNR), is an order doctors write when they and the patient, or advocate have agreed not to use cardiopulmonary resuscitation (CPR) if the heart stops. The term "DNR" makes families focus on what they will *not* do instead of outlining what we *will* do to preserve comfort, dignity, and quality of life. When doctors describe useless end-of-life care like CPR as a *do not* (DNR), families may feel they have chosen to refuse a treatment that could prevent death.

Instead, doctors should discuss a comfort-care course when CPR and other drastic treatments can no longer offer a cure. To help families avoid feeling that they have given up, I often tell them, "instead of doing *'that'* (extreme, high-tech treatments) we will do *'this'* (pain control, other physical comforts, pleasant memories, and dignity). Families understood that we were not doing "nothing." They understood that everyone was still working hard to give their loved one appropriate care.

"Allow Natural Death" (AND)[34], is a more appropriate term. AND focuses on what we *do*, rather than what we *do not*. If the healthcare profession fully adopts the term "AND," more families will feel better about choosing the comfort care course when appropriate.

### Advance Directives: *How Do You Want to Live?*

Parents or legal guardians have the right to make healthcare decisions for people who are underage. Once a person reaches legal age (which depends on the state where they live), no other adult has the right to make these decisions unless the person gives written permission, or a judge gives this authority in a guardianship hearing.

The documents that transfer decision-making power for health decisions are *advance directives*. While you are still healthy, you prepare documents to *direct* your doctors and family in *advance* (before an illness interferes with your ability to make decisions about your healthcare). The documents do not specify an age, a type of illness, or the length of disability. Whether the condition is mental or physical, related to an injury or toxic substance, temporary or permanent, an advance directive records an adult's wishes and puts them into place when she cannot make her wishes known. Advance directives are not concerned with death. They outline the conditions under which you would want to live.

### *Advance Directives Keep You in Control*

These documents ensure that your doctors and family understand your wishes when you can no longer voice them. The advance directive puts someone you trust (your advocate or agent) in charge but only if you cannot demonstrate that you understand your options, can weigh the results of each choice, and communicate your preference.

Your wishes override your agent and the document. If you can make sounds, write, point to words, blink, nod, or give any other gesture to convey clear, consistent communication, you are in charge. These documents do not lock you into your initial decision or limit your choices. You have the right to change or revoke your advance directive at any time.

### *Without Advance Directives, Painful Confusion Reigns*

Questions about decision-making authority can result in court battles and irreversible family discord.

\*\*\*\*\*\*\*\*\*\*\*\*\*\*\*\*\*\*\*\*\*\*\*\*\*\*\*\*\*\*\*\*

One of the most heartbreaking situations I have encountered involved Angela and Hester. They had been a couple for over forty years and neither had executed an advance directive or a will. (This was prior to legislation that allows gay people to marry.) Angela was dying of a terminal illness and Hester was a long-term, loving caregiver. Because there was not an advance directive, doctors turned to the "next of kin," Angela's brother. He disagreed with the couple's lifestyle and because of this had been estranged from Angela for decades. Angela was too ill to execute an advance directive and with death closing in, there was no time for Hester to pursue guardianship.

Angela's brother excluded Hester from all decisions, from Angela's bedside, and from the funeral. Since there was no will, Hester was not entitled to a share of Angela's assets and she had to suffer a long, expensive court battle to claim her share of the assets they had accumulated together. This couple faced death without any ability to comfort each other or even to say "goodbye." Hester grieved alone and faced an economic crisis.

✳✳✳✳✳✳✳✳✳✳✳✳✳✳✳✳✳✳✳✳✳✳✳✳✳✳✳✳✳✳✳

In another sad situation, Mr. Gregory left Mississippi and spent the next thirty years raising a new family in Chicago (without benefit of divorce and remarriage). As he lay dying, his legal wife came up from the South, excluded his Midwestern "wife" and children from his bedside, and made healthcare decisions with which his Chicago family did not agree. Mr. Gregory died while they considered guardianship. Because Mr. Gregory had no will, after the state took its portion, the legal Mrs. Gregory and her adult children inherited everything. The Chicago family got nothing except heartache and legal fees.

✳✳✳✳✳✳✳✳✳✳✳✳✳✳✳✳✳✳✳✳✳✳✳✳✳✳✳✳✳✳✳

In each of these vignettes, an advance directive would have decreased family suffering. Previously uninvolved relatives would not have been able to step in, take control, and exclude the real family. (A will could have protected their financial security though it might not have avoided legal fees.)

Many people believe a spouse automatically has decision-making authority however, a marriage license is not a power of attorney. When there is no advance directive, healthcare professionals usually turn to the legal spouse or the ranking adult relative. The surrogate decision-maker statute in your state outlines the rank-order. You may be surprised by whom your state considers "next of kin."

When there is not an advance directive and doctors speak with a spouse or other family member, this is a courtesy, not a legal status. If any other adult relative disagrees with the decision, the dissatisfied relative can initiate a court battle. These proceedings are expensive and painful. They can also cause treatment delays that either interfere with the loved one's recovery or prolong his suffering.

Some people believe the executor of a will has automatic power of attorney. This is not true. Wills give directions for handling your affairs after you die; they have no power before death. As wills have no power before death, advance directives and the advocate have no power after death.

Advance directives ensure that your last days go the way you want. The documents also protect your family. In those last days, your loved ones are likely to be consumed with grief, guilt, and fear; they will have to make complex and frightening decisions in a highly emotional state. Hearing your directions, even in writing can give them confidence and comfort.

Some relatives fight through their loved one's last days and threaten the family the senior lived to create. Do you think these fights lead to happy holiday celebrations in the future? Advance directives can avoid confusion and fighting because the advocate can say, "This is what Mom wanted." and follow her directions.

*Advance Directive Documents*

### Living Will and the Durable Power of Attorney for Healthcare

Living Wills become active only when the person is near death. They also give specific directions, for example, "If I am too sick to speak for myself, and I am dying, do A, B, and C; don't do D, E, or F."

The Living Will applies only if you are sick enough to die. This document has no meaning if your illness is reversible or if doctors do not expect the condition to cause immediate death. This type of advance directive is equally ineffective if you give directions about "A" to "F" and "G" happens.

A Durable Power of Attorney for Healthcare (POA) is more flexible. The POA allows you to choose someone you trust (agent) to make decisions for you. Most forms do not require your agent's signature and while you should discuss your wishes with the agent, the POA does not require that you do so. The agent doesn't even have to know you have chosen her. (I have known several agents who were blind-sided by the responsibility.) Neither does the agent have to accept the role. This is another reason to discuss your decisions with your agent in advance. If the person you choose does not want the responsibility, you can choose another. It also makes sense to list alternate agents in case someone has a change of heart or is unable to accept the responsibility.

Whether your agent has advance notice or not, by accepting the responsibility, the agent makes a legal contract to follow *your* wishes, not his own. Therefore, the POA document should also describe the kinds of decisions you would want your agent to make. For example, if you could not eat or breathe on your own, would you want doctors to keep you alive on machines? What other treatments are important to you? Which procedures would you rather avoid?

Your agent is in charge only while you cannot make decisions. As soon as you can communicate your wishes in any way and show that you understand your options, your agent has no further authority. If you worry that your agent might take control before it is necessary, you can state in the document that a physician must confirm your disability in writing before your agent can act.

### POLST, Portable Medical Orders

In the 1990s, doctors in Oregon developed POLST (previously called the Physician [or Provider] Order for Life-Sustaining Treatment) to give physicians a comprehensive, yet simple, framework for discussing end-of-life treatments with patients and families. Most states have some form of POLST legislation though each state may use a different name.

Healthcare professionals and emergency response personnel often fear malpractice suits and some have ignored advance directive documents. POLST$_{(35)}$ addresses this issue by documenting decisions in a medical order that these professionals are much less likely to ignore.

Instead of focusing only on CPR, POLST allows adults to record specific decisions about many kinds of treatments available at the end of life. These include but are not limited to feeding tubes, different types of breathing machines, intravenous fluids, antibiotics and other medicines, chemotherapy, and surgery. If you would accept a treatment, the POLST form also allows you to say how long and under what conditions you would be willing to use that treatment. POLST works with your current advance directive without replacing it.

### *How to Prepare and Use an Advance Directive*

Most states require a lawyer to prepare financial powers of attorney, but this is not necessary for healthcare advance directives. You can get forms from hospitals, doctors' offices, senior centers, home-health companies, and area agencies on aging. You can also find your state's forms on the Internet and download them for free. Other services allow you to complete the form online and print it out, but make sure you look for and understand any fees first.

Your advance directive should stay in your medical record and follow you throughout the healthcare system. Unfortunately, this may not happen. Health systems often lose the documents, especially when people move between care sites: home to paramedics, paramedics to the emergency room, emergency room to the hospital, hospital to nursing facility, or back home. Expect this problem and make sure you always have several copies in the medical information binder you take to any care site. (*See Chapter 4: Don't Despair- There IS Help, Bernie Ryan's Binder*)

Give copies of your advance directive to your doctor and all interested family members. Be sure the copies you keep for yourself, give to your agent, and keep with your attorney have original signatures. I learned this the hard way. My mother gave my brother and me power of attorney for health and finance. I needed to access my mother's safe deposit box during her illness. The bank would not allow me to open the box because I had only copies of Mother's Power of Attorney documents. The ones with original signatures were in the safe deposit box!

Make sure you have easy access to copies of your advance directive to instruct paramedics in an emergency. (See the earlier discussion about POLST.) Make sure to review your wishes with your doctor at least yearly to be sure the form reflects your current decisions.

*Which Documents Do You Need? What Happens if You Don't Have One?*

Most people will not need a living will, a power of attorney for healthcare, and a POLST, though if you travel frequently all three documents may be useful. The laws covering the use of these documents may vary in different locations. Before you travel, find out which advance directives apply in the states or countries you visit.

As I said earlier, when people do not choose an advocate, they become disabled with no one to speak for them. Each state has healthcare surrogacy laws to allow relatives ("next of kin") to make decisions. In life-threatening situations, when there is no legal advocate and no family (or no one can find them), two physicians may sign to approve treatment, *even if they've never seen you before.*

No one can predict disability! *Everyone* should give *someone* written permission to make healthcare decisions in case they cannot. Don't wait until you can't participate in your care plan. By then, it will be too late to give directions to someone you trust; you will have no control over which family members or which doctors control your life.

When it comes to healthcare decisions, it doesn't matter if you die; it matters if you don't. Advance directives are not about dying; they are about how you want to live.

## Hospice: "…To Transform Dying into the Last Act of Living Well" —Motto of the VITAS Hospice Charitable Fund

Hospice care provides comfort and dignity to people with incurable illnesses. This program also helps caregivers through their loved one's illness and continues to support families through the grieving process after the loved one passes on. One would think suffering families would rush to participate in such a wonderful service. Unfortunately, hospice care is woefully underutilized. Hospice professionals agree that only about one-third of people eligible for hospice services ever enroll in the program.

Most families believe hospice provides only cancer-care but people with any terminal illness can benefit. End-stage Alzheimer's disease and other dementias, stroke, Parkinson's disease, and end-stage diseases of the heart, lung, liver, and kidney are among the other hospice-appropriate illnesses.

Many doctors and families believe people must be at death's door before they can enroll in hospice. This misunderstanding brings most patients into hospice only in the last days of life; they miss weeks or months of supportive care.

To qualify for hospice care, your doctor signs orders that say you have a terminal illness that is likely to cause death within six months. This is a billing issue, not a clinical one. Even though doctors give estimates, no one can predict the exact length of life for any condition.

The hospice option is appropriate when it becomes clear that drastic treatments may delay but cannot stop an illness from claiming a person's life. Hospice is especially appropriate when treatments are likely to prolong suffering. Some families feel guilty when they enroll their loved ones in hospice because they think it means giving up and doing nothing. This could not be further from the truth.

### Not Intensive Care - Intensively Caring

Families that choose hospice understand they are not going to win the game so they change the rules. Since *cure* is not possible, these families and hospice teams focus on *care*. The teams include nurses, aides, clergy, volunteers, social workers, doctors, and advance practice professionals. The care is very active. However, the team members do nothing *to* your loved one that will not do something *for* her. Instead of painful, drastic treatments that will not stop the cancer, cure the heart failure, or keep the illness from claiming a life, hospice offers an active comfort-care course, which controls pain, eases breathing, and manages other sources of discomfort. Hospice teams support dignity, and provide respect, love, and pleasure. They also support families and continue to work with them for about a year after the loved one dies. My family had several wonderful experiences with hospice.

\*\*\*\*\*\*\*\*\*\*\*\*\*\*\*\*\*\*\*\*\*\*\*\*\*\*

My mother's youngest brother was James Cothran whom his childhood friends called "the Deacon" or "Deak" (because my grandparents made him spend so much time in church). The name stuck with him throughout his life. Uncle Deak always kept an open, wide-mouthed mason jar full of iced tea, punch, or juice in the refrigerator; you risked your life to touch it. Other than that, he was very easy-going. He called all the women and girls in the family "Chicken." When I graduated from medical school, he started calling me "Dr. Chicken."

Uncle Deak ended his journey in hospice care with prostate cancer in 1985. Like many people with terminal cancer, my uncle no longer wanted to eat. Food is love in our family (as it is in many others). My aunts were frustrated and hurt because my uncle could tolerate only a taste of the favorite foods they prepared for him with such love.

Uncle Deak was a jazz fan; instead of forcing him to eat, the hospice team advised my aunts to bring tapes of his favorite artists (he especially loved the work of our cousin, trumpeter, Lee Morgan.) Uncle Deak enjoyed the music and reminisced with friends and family about the good times the music recalled for him. Finally, he slipped away to the sounds he loved.

\*\*\*\*\*\*\*\*\*\*\*\*\*\*\*\*\*\*\*\*\*\*\*\*\*\*

My family also enjoyed the support and services of the hospice program for the last six months of my mother's life.

In March 2003, it became clear that Mother was entering the final phase of her ten-year battle with Alzheimer's disease; further testing or treatments could not change her future. My family enrolled her in hospice and immediately found ourselves wrapped in the warm blanket that is VITAS Innovative Hospice Care, Inc. Although it was not the intensive care unit (ICU), it was intensive care. The nurse, aide, social worker, and chaplain saw Mother several times each week; they contacted me just as often. When Mother's time drew near, she went into "Crisis Care," and an aide was with us around the clock for the last eighteen hours. The aide stayed in the background and she responded quickly when any need arose. She kept Mother's mouth moist and provided other care to keep her comfortable. She also took care of me. When I knelt at Mother's side, the aide gave me a pillow to kneel on. She said, "Without this, you won't be able to stay down there as long as you want to."

Nearby family members came to say good-bye and others called from around the country. I held the phone to Mother's ear so she could hear loving voices wishing her a good journey. I sang "Swing Low Sweet Chariot" and lifted my head off Mother's chest a moment before she took her last breath. She stepped on the chariot and left the planet. It was the most peaceful and beautiful Homegoing I have ever been honored to witness.

In 2009 and 2011, both my mother's oldest sister, Aunt Laura, and her oldest brother, Sam (whom everybody called "Uncle"), passed away peacefully in hospice. Both were in their nineties.

Why has my family been so blessed by the hospice experience when so many other families miss this opportunity? *We did not deny that our loved ones were dying.*

After Uncle Deak passed, Uncle (the oldest of the Cothran siblings), thanked me for telling the family the truth. He said, "You prepared us and told us about hospice. If you hadn't, we would have kept on thinking Deak was gonna get better. It would have been a real shock when he passed."

Because our family opted for hospice care in the face of incurable illnesses, my mother, aunt, and uncles slipped into eternity without panic, poking, or prodding. Our family had the opportunity to love them…to death. That's what hospice is.

*What is Palliative Care?*

Since the late 1980s, the concept of palliative care has emerged from the umbrella of hospice care. Both services support people with chronic illnesses that will eventually cause death. The hallmarks of both fields are quality of life: pain control, dignity, emotional and spiritual support. Hospice intervenes only when the end is unavoidable and expected within six months. There is no time limit for palliative care. A palliative care consultation can bring great benefits as soon as doctors diagnose a serious, chronic illness or at any time along the care path.

Doctors, healthcare staff, families, anyone can request a palliative care consultation. With palliative care, people can still choose aggressive therapies. However, at each decision point, the person, family, primary care physician, consultants, and the palliative care team have proactive discussions about:

- How much benefit could a specific test or treatment offer compared to the discomfort it might cause?

- Which treatments would a person want to undergo and which would she decide against?

- How long would he wish to try a specific procedure?

- What factors will she consider when making decisions as new options arise?

- When do we say "when?" What symptoms or test results would prompt a doctor to recommend or the person or family to request comfort care only?

- What concerns and values do the person and family have about the end-of-life transition?

In 2006, the American Board of Medical Specialists made Hospice and Palliative Care a fully board-certified subspecialty (like cardiology). Doctors who have completed medical school and residency programs must complete an additional two-year advanced training program. Only then can they take the certifying examination in hospice and palliative care.

While I am grateful for these professionals, I am sorry the field of medicine needed a separate subspecialty for care at the end of life. I wish all doctors learned to make quality of life a priority and consider whether we *should* use all treatments just because we *can*. I wish the training of doctors emphasized discussing priorities and values with patients and families. I want all health care professionals to understand that we have never had control over life and death. Our responsibility is to use science only as long as it can offer the best chance for the quality of life a person chooses.

We are also responsible to stay involved to support and comfort patients and families when illness steals that chance. That is our job. It is also our privilege. I am honored that families have trusted me to walk with them at such a stressful and poignant time.

Studies report that the time doctors spend in direct contact with patients is about fifteen minutes. [36] Even so, that is not enough time to walk a family through end-of-life decisions, especially if there are problems with communication or brain function.

Caregivers should schedule conferences and health insurance companies should reimburse doctors for this extra time. In the 2008 presidential campaign, some politicians inflamed fears with media clips that said legislation to allow insurance coverage for discussions of hospice care was "pulling the plug on grandma." In fact, the goal was to extend health insurance coverage so *all* families could have un-rushed, compassionate time to discuss all care options. Without insurance coverage, access to these critical conferences is limited to families that can afford to pay out-of-pocket.

Even if doctors make time for these discussions, many do not know how to do so. Many try but can use only flimsy words like "She's failing," instead of coming right out to say, "He's dying." My program, "How to Give Bad News," teaches health professionals and clergy how to set up the appropriate environment, use clear and compassionate language, handle conflict and other strong emotions, document what happened during the conference, and arrange effective follow-up.

Even though some medical schools and residency training programs offer seminars on communication, many doctors just cannot have this discussion. If your doctors seem to believe death is failure, if they keep ordering tests and scheduling procedures without discussing the risks and benefits, *be confident*. Ask, "How will we use this information to help her? Will this plan help her get back to [insert your loved one's favorite activity]?" You have the right to ask about hospice and palliative care, request a referral, or contact these programs yourself. The information these professionals offer will help you have more effective conversations with your doctor.

I look forward to the day when everyone can accept that there are worse things than dying (like suffering). In some situations, death is unavoidable, and we should not *try* to avoid it. Even if death is not the most pressing issue, quality of life should always be the goal.

## The Priority Should Always Be Quality of Life

Prior to surgery or other major procedures, doctors ask patients and families to give "informed consent." When you sign these documents, you agree that you and the doctor have discussed all the options and you agree to have a specific treatment. You say that you understand all the dangers involved: including possible bleeding, infections, or injuries, and the risk of more serious conditions, emergency procedures, and death.

I think informed consent should also include the risk of chronic disability. Shifts in blood pressure or complications of anesthesia could make an otherwise healthy older person survive surgery only to live confused and dependent for the last months of life. If a senior knew this upfront, she might decide not to have open-heart surgery to replace a diseased valve. Instead of risking life with disability, he might prefer to go on with his usual activities and risk an abnormal heart rhythm and sudden death. A person has the right to understand ALL risks and decide on a course that respects his values.

\*\*\*\*\*\*\*\*\*\*\*\*\*\*\*\*\*\*\*\*\*\*\*\*\*\*\*\*\*\*\*

I shared this opinion about a broader definition of "informed consent" with a surgical colleague who disagreed. He said, "When you need surgery, you need it. There's no option." I responded, "That's because your idea of success is getting off the operating table; mine is getting back on the golf course or back in the kitchen baking sweet potato pies."

\*\*\*\*\*\*\*\*\*\*\*\*\*\*\*\*\*\*\*\*\*\*\*\*\*\*\*\*\*\*\*

There are times when a person understands the risks and decides to take them. That is also the person's right.

\*\*\*\*\*\*\*\*\*\*\*\*\*\*\*\*\*\*\*\*\*\*\*\*\*\*\*\*\*\*\*

Mr. Dean was a seventy-nine-year-old hunter and farmer who had survived cancer of the prostate and colon as well as several heart attacks. He also lived with chronic lung disease and congestive heart failure. Over a period of years, he developed severe, chronic pain in his back and leg because of pinched nerves from arthritis in his spine. In addition to the usual conversations about bleeding, infection, emergencies and death, the neurosurgeon and I were honest with Mr. Dean about the possible impact of anesthesia and surgical complications on his lungs, heart, brain, and kidneys. We included the possibility that he might not be able to breathe on his own and might have permanent confusion. Mr. Dean said, "Doc, I'll take those odds; if I have to live another day with this pain, I'm going out behind the barn with one of my guns."

We did the surgery. Although Mr. Dean had several complications, one close call with breathing problems, and a bout of severe confusion, he came through and lived another seven years. Despite mild memory loss, he was able to ride his tractor around his farm, pain-free, as he had wished. He took a risk; it was his right and his call.

*******************************

Professionals in hospice and palliative care are not alone in their dedication to quality of life. Others have become more sensitive to this issue including: patients and families, other healthcare professionals, clergy, other community leaders, members of the media, and professionals in law and business. I have heard many concerned people say, "It's not what's the matter with them; it's what *matters* to them." Even though some of the coming changes in healthcare financing support this concept, we aren't there yet. Until our health system emphasizes quality of life and ensures that all health professionals are trained in hospice and palliative care principles, I'm glad there are specialists in this important area.

In the first section, you learned that the twenty-first century Crisis in Caregiving has made your caregiving more difficult than it was for your parents and grandparents. The second section showed you how to get the help you need and encouraged you to protect yourself. The third section recommended ways to protect your physical, financial, emotional and spiritual health. The fourth section reviewed how to get through some of the most difficult decisions. Now that you are an expert caregiver, the fifth and final section will show you how to advocate for effective changes in public policy that affect your senior and other caregivers.

# SECTION V

# From Advocacy to Activism

**We Need Your Help with Public Policy**

Health professionals, administrators, and legislators are working to help our nation meet the needs of seniors and other citizens who live with chronic illness. Please understand that:

- They cannot do this without your help.
- You can be effective advocates for change or stand in the gap until the change comes.
- You know exactly what you need to make your own caregiving easier.
- You will not be able to affect the system unless you understand how and why it is broken.
- You can turn this information into action by direct contact with your legislators and by working with organizations that advocate for laws that support more effective health care policies.

# CHAPTER 17

# Paying for Eldercare: Follow the Money

### Demographics Don't Drive the Dollars

The first Baby Boomers reached age seventy in 2016. With this massive group of adults firmly in the senior ranks, one would think affordable senior services would be plentiful. This is not the case.

For example, adult day services could be a Godsend to caregivers. This resource fits into the new health system's goals for community-based care, and it is less expensive than assisted-living facilities or nursing homes (about seventy-five dollars per day versus several hundreds of dollars per day).

In the first edition, I cited a Robert Wood Johnson Foundation survey of adult day centers in the United States. Twenty-three of the fifty states offered less than thirty percent of the required adult day services (based on the estimated population of disabled seniors). Only six states approached seventy percent of the need; this group included the smallest states (Rhode Island) and states with relatively few seniors (Alaska and Hawaii.)[37] The follow-up study did not update those specific statistics. It did report that the number of people using adult day services had increased by sixty-five percent and the number of centers increased by thirty-three percent since between 2002 and 2010.[38] I did not find more recent data, however, many state and municipal governments face budget crises. Private companies also face funding challenges. I cannot believe the resources will keep up with the number of Baby Boomers who may need adult day services.

In my area, several centers have closed, and I haven't seen any new ones open. I spoke with several of the eldercare consultants who worked with me when I was in practice, and they confirmed that there are fewer adult day centers now. Some said the loss of adult day care services has forced them to give up suggesting that option to their clients.

It would make sense to improve funding for adult day care centers. Most caregivers cobble together a care system using family, friends, hired caregivers, and community services that last only for a time. The government could spend less money on institutions if caregivers could routinely access adult day services for at least a few hours per day as part of these piecemeal care systems.

## The Eldercare Workforce: High Turnover Hurts Everyone

Despite the growing number of seniors, the number of workers available to provide personal care is shrinking. In part, this is due to the high turnover rates among these workers. All articles I reviewed on Long-term Care Facility (LTC) staff reports that high turnover has a negative effect on facility costs and residents' care. Facilities pay to recruit, interview, and train new employees, and residents suffer more infections, transfers to hospitals, and other indications of care quality (perhaps due to staff with less experience). These reports also agree that the high turnover affects residents' comfort and quality of life when they grieve relationships with departed staff and have frequent exposure to unfamiliar workers.

Since the first edition, the salaries of nursing home aides and community care workers have increased a few dollars above the wages of fast-food workers.[39] However, like other low-wage workers, few facility caregivers have pensions or other benefits; before the Affordable Care Act, most had no health insurance. Even today, it is not clear what percentage of these workers have access to affordable benefit packages.

Despite low wages and questionable benefits, the work is much harder. Aides feed, groom, lift, bathe, and change diapers for sick adults. Many patients cannot assist in their own care; some are not very pleasant, either because of their illnesses or because their disabilities frustrate them. Training to cope with these challenges is inconsistent at best.

The certification requirements for direct-care workers are minimal and there is not a national standard. Most nursing homes do not have large training budgets. Large companies that operate several nursing homes can invest in extensive, company-wide staff training that may decrease staff turnover. Unfortunately, turnover rates can still affect these educational programs. Many years ago, I served as the education director for a long-term care facility that was dedicated to training. Three months into the first series of seminars, new employees made up almost 100 per cent of the class. Instead of moving the training plan forward, I had to start the program from the beginning.

Despite low wages, questionable benefit packages, and limited training, I have worked with so many capable, dedicated direct-care workers. They do exemplary jobs, put in extra unpaid hours, and even spend their own money to supplement supplies. A recent study of nursing home staff turnover suggests that feeling undervalued, poorly supported, and having a poor relationship with management may have a larger impact on turnover than working conditions or wages.[40] We need more research to explore the financial, job-satisfaction, and administrative reasons for LTC staff turnover so these facilities can implement changes to improve the work experience and give seniors the high quality of care that they deserve.

## Picking Caregivers' Pockets

Family caregivers provide over seventy percent of the eldercare in this country, and they do it for free. The estimated value of this "donated" care is over $470 billion per year. This is more than Medicare, private insurance, and public aid pay hospitals, home health agencies, and nursing homes. [41] These numbers consider only direct-care costs. They do not begin to assess the financial impact of lost wages, smaller bonuses, missed promotions, and decreased retirement savings.

Poor performance evaluations caused by coming to work late, leaving early, missing days, or being distracted at work (presenteeism) can put caregivers' income and even their jobs at risk. Even if a caregiver keeps her position, she may risk current and future income by choosing caregiving over the extra work that leads to (and comes from) promotions. (*See Chapter 10: Protect Your Financial Health - Protect Your Income*). Although other caregivers worry about hiring strangers and choose early retirement to give care themselves, it is not clear that early retirement is always a choice. It is difficult to know whether work-related disciplinary actions (or the perceived threat of these actions) influence these decisions.

Caregivers also incur expenses. The average family caregiver spends about $5500 per year out-of-pocket to supplement seniors' finances: food, copayments, hired help, medicine, household expenses, and other necessities. For long-distance caregivers, that sum increases to about $9,000 (and may not include travel expenses).(42) Most dipped into savings, changed lifestyle, reduced working hours, or retired to give care.(43)

\*\*\*\*\*\*\*\*\*\*\*\*\*\*\*\*\*\*\*\*\*\*\*\*\*\*\*\*\*\*\*\*

Miss Brown was the youngest of her parents' three children. Her brothers married and moved out while she remained her parents' primary support. She pursued an accounting career. Her mother handled physical care when Miss Brown's father became ill, and Miss Brown supplemented her parents' limited finances. She cosigned when they could not qualify for a mortgage on a new home and she made most of the payments. After Miss Brown's father died, her mother developed dementia and needed twenty-four-hour supervision. The state-supported community care program offered a worker for three hours per day, four days per week. Miss Brown's mother needed eight to twelve hours of care during the day, and the community care program would not allow the workers to work for her on their own. Private care agencies would not accept the minimum wages paid by the state, and Miss Brown could not afford to cover the extra hours. She spent every evening and weekend as the sole caregiver.

In nine years of care, Miss Brown estimates she spent about $350,000 on hired care in the community and one year contributing to nursing home costs. She could not estimate the clothing, personal items, medicines, and copayments that came directly from her paycheck. Expenses also used up her savings and much of her pension money for which she paid penalties and fees for early withdrawal.

Now, Miss Brown is seventy-five years old with arthritis and other health problems. She has no children and her one remaining sibling has his own health challenges. Miss Brown worked full time until two years ago when she was laid off from her job. She struggles to maintain her Medicare supplemental health insurance and other costs of living.

\*\*\*\*\*\*\*\*\*\*\*\*\*\*\*\*\*\*\*\*\*\*\*\*\*\*\*\*\*\*\*\*

America is poised to create another generation of impoverished, health-challenged seniors as caregivers exhaust their savings to pay for others' care. Like Miss Brown, many leave the workforce before retirement age to provide care. The average caregiver is well under age sixty-five and may incur significant penalties for withdrawals from retirement investments. Other caregivers have minimal retirement resources because they:

- Worked for companies that did not offer a pension plan
- Worked part-time and did not qualify for pension benefits
- Earned low wages and did not accrue significant pension funds
- Spent less time in the workforce due to child-rearing, caregiving, or illness and
- Did not work long enough to be vested in the pension fund nor
- Work enough quarters to qualify for maximum benefits under Social Security

Limited retirement resources may impose the additional burden of being too small to support life, yet too large to allow access to public assistance programs. Early retirees are usually too young for Medicare; before the Affordable Care Act, many did not have health insurance.

## Medicare Pays to Do Things *to* People Not *for* People

Congress enacted Medicare in the 1960s, at the end of the era of acute illnesses that either kill people quickly or get better right away. Though chronic conditions had begun to challenge the health system, with increasing demands for care over time, legislators still designed Medicare to support procedures, treatments, and technology focused on cure. The twenty-first century is the era of incurable chronic conditions, which continue despite high-tech machines and invasive treatments. Medicare has yet to catch up. Medicare will pay for a CT scan or MRI of the head as many times as a doctor orders one of these tests because of "changes in mental status." Even though Medicare is a national program, if a senior had an MRI in another hospital, there is no easy way for a doctor to get the results or even to know the other test occurred. The system does not issue these alerts in the same city, let alone between different parts of the country. Some systems do not flag duplicate services in the same health system.

Medicare usually covers the cost of these extra tests without question, yet it does not support the time a doctor sits with a family to explain, "The problem is Alzheimer's disease. Another brain scan will not change your loved one's condition. This is what we can do to take care of her."

Proposed changes in healthcare legislation might offer some support for patient education time. Even so, Medicare still will not pay for other services that could support wellness and avoid hospital stays. These services include:

- Assistance with personal care, transportation or managing finances and medicines.
- Housekeeping, shopping, cooking, or other chore services.
- Adult day services or companions.
- Transportation (except in an emergency or moving between hospitals and long-term care facilities).

In 2015, Congress repealed the Sustainable Growth Rate (SGR) calculation, a complex formula that mandated regular cuts in payments to doctors and hospitals, despite increasing demands for care. Congress replaced SGR with the Medicare Assessment and CHIP Reauthorization Act of 2015 (MACRA).

The new legislation incorporates several ways to decide the level of payment based on quality of care, effective use of electronic medical records, and improving office practice protocols. Even if doctors give high quality care, many are not used to recording their thoughts and care plans in computers. Few have learned how to provide the detail that new documentation guidelines require. Since the new system also requires more regulations and paperwork, doctors hire extra staff and spend less time with patients. Doctors are frustrated and some bail out of Medicare[44] and other insurance plans because of:

- The financial stress of increased practice overhead (staff and non-patient care time) and decreased income
- Frustration from the lack of training on effective record-keeping, and compliance with regulations
- Decreased job satisfaction after spending years and hundreds of thousands of dollars to learn patient-care, only to do more paperwork.

Medical conferences and hospital doctors' lounges are abuzz with conversations about dropping out of Medicare, other insurance plans, and out of medical practice all together. If our health system wants to keep up with the needs of older adults and the chronically ill and also promote wellness for everyone, this will have to change.

## All You Have is Medicare? You're Uninsured!

The following numbers are current for 2020. Please check www.medicare.gov every year.

Medicare Part A covers hospice and skilled care from home health agencies and nursing homes (See the section below on Nursing Home Financing). It also covers inpatient hospital services. After a person pays a $1,408 deductible, Part A requires no other copayments for the first sixty hospital days. Days sixty-one through ninety carry a $352 daily copayment. A daily $704 copayment applies from day ninety-one up to a lifetime maximum of another sixty days. After that, the patient pays all costs.

Part B covers outpatient care including visits to doctors' offices and urgent care centers, tests, surgeries, and other procedures that happen in the outpatient setting. Out-of-pocket costs include a monthly premium of $144.60 (which can be higher based on income). There is also an annual deductible of $198 after which Medicare pays eighty percent of the outpatient charges. Outpatient services include care in the emergency room and in the hospital under observation care. Doctors place a person in observation when the illness is serious enough to need a hospital stay but not serious enough for care to be medically necessary beyond two midnights. This can be confusing. Though people in emergency rooms and in observation are physically in the hospital, Medicare covers these services as outpatient, under Part B. Also, since few hospitals have separate observation areas, two people may share a room, eat the same food, and wear hospital gowns yet one is an inpatient and the other is in observation.

One of the stated goals of the new health insurance financing plan is to shift care from high-cost inpatient areas to lower-cost outpatient sites when safe and appropriate. Hospitals face financial penalties when they discharge a patient and readmit him for the same illness within thirty days. Instead of calling this rebound care a "readmission," to avoid the penalties, some hospital place people in observation and try to extend the observation period to several days. Hospitals can convert observation to inpatient status but only when they can document that the illness and care plan are serious enough that the higher care is medically necessary. Medicare and insurance companies review the medical records and if they determine that inpatient care was not medically necessary, Medicare denies inpatient coverage under Part A. It pays only eighty percent of the cost under Part B, and the patient is on the hook for twenty percent of every hospital charge, every aspirin (and other medicines,) doctor visit, test, treatment, and procedure. Twenty percent of several thousand dollars is out of reach for many seniors and their families.

In 2016, Congress passed legislation that requires a hospital to inform people whether they are in observation or inpatient status. Before that, most people were not aware they were in observation and at discharge, the hospital would present a huge bill to the unsuspecting person. Medical bills are the primary cause of bankruptcy in the US overall and are major contributors to senior poverty.

To avoid huge financial burdens from medical bills, seniors must have Medicare and either supplemental insurance, an employer-based plan, or a Medicare Advantage (Part C) plan to cover some or all out-of-pocket costs.

Under Part C, Medicare partners with manage care companies to cover Part A and B services and the copayments. Some plans also cover prescription medicine. Medicare Advantage plans usually offer extra benefits including preventive dental and vision care, hearing aids, fitness clubs, and other services. Some plans require a monthly amount in addition to the Part B premium that Medicare deducts from your Social Security check. Other plans do not. Both types of plans may charge additional costs. Some Part C contracts require you to choose doctors, hospitals, and test sites from a specific network and request referrals for procedures, and care from specialists. Others allow you to choose any doctor or care site without referrals regardless of network. Some plans include these out-of-network choices without additional payments. Others charge copayments in either a fixed dollar amount or as a percentage of the total cost.

*Learn How the Plans Work.*
When you choose a Part C plan, you agree to let the insurance company manage your Medicare benefits. *You must behave as if you do not have Medicare.* When you go to a hospital, office, or another care site, show the receptionist your insurance company identification card. Do not present your red, white, and blue Medicare card. If the care team bills Medicare, the government will deny payment. If your Part C plan requires referrals and you did not have one, the insurance company won't pay either. You will.

If you have Medicare and health coverage from a current or past employer, Medicare is primary for some care services. This means that the care team should bill Medicare first, and the other plan will pick up the copayments. For other types of care and other care locations, your employer-based plan is primary.

The number of plans and different combinations of costs, benefits, networks, and primary payment responsibility can be mind-boggling. To avoid unexpected out-of-pocket costs, piles of paperwork, and communication nightmares, be sure you understand who pays for what and where. Beware of mail and phone calls from agents who represent a specific plan or earn commissions by finding a plan for you. AARP, area agencies on aging, and medicare.gov have clearly written materials that discuss the different parts of Medicare. They have objective information about how to choose the best supplement or Part C plan for you, and they can help you understand how all plans work with Medicare Part D (This is the prescription drug plan. Medicare charges penalties if you don't chose a plan that includes drug coverage.) Many local social service agencies offer counselors who can walk you through the decision process for little or no cost.

**Nursing Home Financing**

Although many caregivers believe Medicare pays for all nursing home expenses, state-supported public aid programs, patients, and their families are the primary payors.

People with Medicare qualify for the long-term care benefit only when:

- They have a "skilled nursing need" (complex treatment plans that require a registered nurse [RN]) for most of the twenty-four hours of every day.

- The person was an inpatient in the hospital for a specific illness and now needs nursing home care for the same condition.

- The medical records confirm that the care plan was medically necessary in the hospital for at least two midnights.

- The inpatient hospital stay occurred within thirty days of the nursing home admission.

*Observation days do not count.* Many people and their families expect Medicare to pay for the nursing home once they leave the hospital only to find that they are not eligible because they were in "observation" status.

If a person does qualify for nursing home care, Medicare pays 100 percent of the cost for the first twenty days. For the next 100 days, Medicare covers all costs except a daily copayment for which the patient or family is responsible. In 2020, this is $176. per day. (You can find annual updates to Medicare benefits and copayments at www.medicare.gov). If you need more than 120 days of nursing home care, Medicare pays *nothing*, even if the senior's condition still meets the requirements for skilled nursing care.

Medicare will support another 120 days of skilled care only if the patient stays out of the hospital and any other Medicare Part A-supported facility (nursing home, rehabilitation center, home health, or hospice) for at least sixty days. The Medicare payment clock does not reset until a person has another qualifying inpatient hospital stay (not observation) and needs skilled nursing care.

When a senior's illnesses are not severe enough to qualify for skilled services or when they need care for more than 120 days, families must either pay privately or apply for public aid.

## Must Seniors Give All Their Money to the Nursing Home?

Nursing home admissions staff review a senior's finances to compute a "spend-down" number. This is what nursing home applicants and their families must pay out-of-pocket before the state will pay for nursing home care.

Families empty bank accounts, spend investments, raid pensions, and deplete other financial resources to meet the spend-down requirement. *They must include any assets transferred out of the senior's name within a specific time-period before the nursing home application.* Each state decides on the spend-down amount and the time period. In the first edition, I told you that the state of Illinois includes any assets transferred in the last thirty-six months. Today, it's five years.

Unless there is a chance that the senior can return home, the state may also place liens against any property. This earmarks money from any future sale to repay what public aid spent on nursing home care. Many families are upset about spending their seniors' resources instead of inheriting them. When they say, "We don't want to give the state all Daddy's money," I ask, "Why shouldn't Daddy's resources pay for *HIS* care?"

## Does That Leave the Healthy Spouse Homeless and Hungry?

When one spouse needs nursing home care and the other does not, families may worry about having enough money to support the healthy spouse in the community. In the past, some couples made the painful decision to split assets in a divorce rather than use all assets to satisfy the spend-down requirement. Today, public aid programs include a "spousal impoverishment" policy. Under this plan, the spend-down figure allows the spouse to keep enough money for burial, as well as the primary home, one car, and a specific amount of income and assets.

This policy applies to any blood relative who lived with the nursing home applicant *and was the primary caregiver* for a specific amount of time. (It does not apply to people who only lived in the house). Each state determines the amount of excluded income and assets, the required length of caregiving, and how they recognize the primary caregiver. Estate planners, attorneys, and social workers can tell you about the current information for your state.

When families do not want to use a nursing home, or their loved ones do not need round-the clock care, many families investigate assisted-living facilities.

# CHAPTER 18

## Assisted-Living Facilities: They Are Not *Always* a Lifeline

NOTE: Some people in the assisted-living industry sent outraged comments about this chapter in the first edition of *To Survive Caregiving*. In the years since the publication of that book, I have cared for many more people in these facilities. I have also performed eldercare consultations for many families who wanted to investigate care options. As I did for the first edition, again I interviewed residents, families, administrators, nurses, and staff in these facilities. Sorry folks, but I have neither experienced, heard, nor seen anything that changes my initial assessment, contradicts the examples I offered in the first edition, or refutes the comments in this second edition.

When families promised never to use a nursing home or feel blindsided by the financial realities of that promise, they often look to assisted-living facilities (ALF) as an alternative to nursing home placement. That is not always a good move.

These programs can be lifesavers when their resources match residents' needs. However, disasters can occur when unrealistic expectations make caregivers overlook some very real limitations in these communities.

## A System Designed for People Who Do Not Exist

ALF administrators often tell me that their residents "just need a little help." In my experience, if that is all they needed, these seniors would still be at home. Either they need more than a little help, the family cannot provide the help they need, or they have no family to help them. I have found that many residents have severe medical problems and need more resources than ALFs were designed to offer. However, administrators and families have powerful incentives to believe these facilities are the right choice.

Admissions counselors around the country admitted that they feel pressure from their employers to fill beds. They may accept residents who are too ill to manage in the environment rather than keep low numbers of residents in the facility. This number is the "census," and it translates into dollars.

Administrators and marketing managers tell me that the current economy and the pandemic also make their jobs more challenging. Families may choose to allow unemployed relatives to provide eldercare at home instead of paying facility fees. This further threatens the census and may increase the pressure to bring in residents. (Administrators of adult day centers report the same challenges. Some non-skilled home care agencies may be doing better as families try to avoid COVID-19 infections in nursing homes).

In defense of the ALF industry, the laws that regulate these communities do not allow them to provide *medical* care. Unfortunately, the questions on most ALF admission forms are too general to detect serious illnesses. For example, dementia is a common, age-related condition in which problems with memory and other brain actions make seniors unsafe at home. The regulations direct ALFs to deny admission to people whose primary diagnosis is dementia. Even so, when I served as the contract physician for ALFs, I saw that many residents took prescription medicines for dementia, yet the diagnosis did not appear in their records.

In the past few years, I have reviewed pre-admission paperwork for new ALF residents and found that most did not include common tests of memory and other brain functions. Families may be so desperate to find a safe care site that they don't volunteer information about memory loss. To protect the census, admissions staff may not ask. Either way, ALFs can admit people with dementia who are not supposed to be there.

\*\*\*\*\*\*\*\*\*\*\*\*\*\*\*\*\*\*\*\*\*\*\*\*\*\*

The financial administrator of an ALF asked me to certify that a resident was mentally capable of managing her money. The state regulations require the resident to understand her rights and responsibilities, renew her contract every year, and assign most of her social security income to the facility. Although the diagnosis of dementia did not appear in her chart, she seemed confused. I performed a common mental status examination, found that she had significant memory loss and instead of signing the form, ordered additional tests. My diagnosis caused an administrative uproar. The administrator said, "Doctor, you don't understand. If she doesn't sign her contract, we will not get paid." I responded, "*You* don't understand. I don't believe this lady knows what she's signing, and bright orange is not my color. I'm not going to jail for fraud."

*******************************

Facilities can perform basic mental status screening, identify potential residents who need more in-depth testing, and require the results before they accept an application. If the facility admits people with dementia or other brain conditions, they can enact policies to identify legal representatives for these residents. These advocates could make decisions on behalf of residents who were physically able to live in the facility but unable to make self-care decisions. Most ALFs have no such policies because *residents are not supposed to have significant memory loss.*

*******************************

One Saturday, a nurse called me about a resident who had moved into the ALF a few days before. The woman had refused to come to the dining area for meals and the housekeeping staff found her on the floor of her apartment screaming and refusing to get up. I arranged for an ambulance to transfer her to the emergency room of a local hospital where the doctors found no evidence of a stroke, problems with medicines, infections, or any other treatable illness. The woman did have profound memory loss (which had not been documented on the facility admission forms), yet her family insisted there had been no change. They said, "That's just Mom's usual forgetfulness." At discharge from the hospital, the woman went to a nursing home where she could receive the level of care and supervision she needed.

*******************************

## Specialized Dementia-Care Assisted-Living

ALFs especially designed for residents with dementia are available, but they are much more expensive than regular facilities (often more than $6,000 per month). Long-term care and supplemental insurance plans may help with the cost while Medicare, private health insurance, and public aid will not. Families must pay out-of-pocket.

Since I published the first edition of this book, many regular ALFs have developed specialized memory units where they give medicine and provide supervision. In my experience, there are still challenges in training staff about dementia. They also need training about how dementia presents and progresses, how to manage common behavioral symptoms, and the ethical and legal factors involved in caring for people who cannot make their own decisions.

\*\*\*\*\*\*\*\*\*\*\*\*\*\*\*\*\*\*\*\*\*\*\*\*

A caregiver in my medical practice admitted her husband to a dementia-specific ALF while she went to their granddaughter's wedding out of state. Confusion is common when people with dementia first leave familiar surroundings. On the first night, the patient became agitated, and the head nurse called to ask me to transfer the patient to the emergency room for intravenous medicine. The nurse was upset because "he's having a "nervous breakdown."

The same facility refused to let a man's grandson take him out to lunch because the man's daughter had arranged the senior's admission to the facility. Although the man clearly had memory loss and he took medicine for dementia, his primary doctor had not documented the diagnosis in his chart. Neither was there legal documentation that the man could not make his own decisions, nor an appointed guardian, nor a power of attorney. The grandson had no less right to his grandfather than the senior's daughter did; the facility had no right to deny the man's request to go out with his grandson. Lawyers got involved.

\*\*\*\*\*\*\*\*\*\*\*\*\*\*\*\*\*\*\*\*\*\*\*\*

## Who Monitors Residents' Health?

Even if residents are totally independent when they come into an ALF, serious illnesses can develop over time. If the facility does not build in a monitoring system, residents can become too ill for the environment, and no one would notice until a disaster struck.

If after years of living in the facility, a resident becomes confused and wanders out of the building, he could die from exposure, get hit by a car, or become a victim of violence. Facilities that are not dementia-focused have neither a plan to diagnose developing confusion nor security measures to prevent wandering *because people in these facilities are not supposed to be confused or to wander.* Even so, people with confusion and behavioral difficulties live in these facilities and can wander out with sad consequences.

In addition to dementia, I found other undiagnosed medical conditions. These would have been simple to treat if the staff had training about common symptoms and policies to alert health care professionals. In medical jargon, WNL means "within normal limits" but in some cases, these letters seem to mean "we never looked."

\*\*\*\*\*\*\*\*\*\*\*\*\*\*\*\*\*\*\*\*\*\*\*\*\*

The staff of one facility thought a resident "complained all the time just to get attention." I found that his joints were red, hot, and swollen with the classic deformities of rheumatoid arthritis. He was in pain! A simple oral medicine relieved his suffering and stopped his "attention-seeking." My examination also uncovered undiagnosed memory loss that made it hard for him to communicate his needs. I transferred him out of the facility to a more appropriate care site.

\*\*\*\*\*\*\*\*\*\*\*\*\*\*\*\*\*\*\*\*\*\*\*\*\*

I do not fault the ALF staff. Most of the aides and nursing assistants are not trained to recognize medical problems. More facilities are beginning to hire registered nurses (RN) however, there may only be one RN in a facility, and that nurse may work part-time. There is usually no professional nursing staff in the evenings or on weekends.

Extra help is available, for a price. Some communities supply aides that families can hire to give personal care. Facilities can also either contract with a nursing agency or allow families to hire private duty nurses from outside. These costs are not included in the basic fees. Although supplemental and long-term care insurance might help, Medicare will not pay for these services at all. If the resident qualifies for skilled nursing care, Medicare will pay for a nurse who usually comes for about a half-hour, three days per week, for only about six weeks. For many families, extra costs overwhelm the budget.

\*\*\*\*\*\*\*\*\*\*\*\*\*\*\*\*\*\*\*\*\*\*\*\*\*\*\*\*\*\*

The daughter of one person in my practice paid these extra costs then wished she had not moved her mother out of her home. "For the money I spend," this caregiver said, "I could have kept her where she was and hired twenty-four-hour care."

\*\*\*\*\*\*\*\*\*\*\*\*\*\*\*\*\*\*\*\*\*\*\*\*\*\*\*\*\*\*

Other facilities have strengthened their professional nursing staff or contracted with physicians and advance practice professionals (nurse practitioners [NP] or physician assistants [PA]) to offer visits on-site. Residents do not have to use these services, and the facilities assume no responsibility for the care. The ALF expects families to take their loved one to a private physician in the community, or work with a doctor who comes to the facility.

Too often, either the senior has no family or the caregivers have breathed sighs of relief, thinking the facility will take care of everything. In other situations, an already stressed caregiver finds herself with the same amount of responsibility that she had before the senior became an ALF resident.

### Who Manages the Medicines?

Although the staff can remind seniors to take their medicine, they cannot give them the pills. Many families come to the facility, fill medicine boxes, and supervise pill-taking themselves. Many ALFs contract with pharmacies that deliver medicines to the facility and provide automatic prescription-refills. Most contract pharmacies protect residents by monitoring for drug interactions, allergies, and medication errors. However, I have not seen many contract pharmacies that send reminders about routine blood tests needed for safe use of some medicines. When I cared for ALF residents, I found several with prescriptions that needed routine tests every one to three months. Some of those residents had not had the necessary blood tests in more than a year. This puts residents at risk of under- or overtreatment and serious medicine side effects.

Though many families take advantage of the convenience of contract pharmacies, facilities cannot require residents to use the services. Families that do not use the ALF pharmacy may shop at several community pharmacies to get the best price (as we all often do). A universal communication system between facilities, doctors, and pharmacies exists for only narcotics (powerful pain medicines with a high risk of addiction and abuse). For other medicines, pharmacy-hopping offers no way to send alerts to protect these residents from overdose, medication errors, drug interactions, or side effects.

Operational and regulatory policies that govern the ALF industry create a medical, financial, ethical, and legal nightmare waiting to happen. The guidelines do not allow the facilities to hire enough professional staff or train them to monitor and treat the residents' *medical* needs. Census-based admissions policies may create conflicts of interest that lead the facilities to admit people whose care needs are greater than the facilities' resources. When people are in the wrong environment, they risk poor health and frequent trips to the hospital. The facilities also risk lawsuits related to legal questions and avoidable accidents and injuries.

### A Safer System

ALFs could request an independent, LOCRx prior to admission. They could also require medical care teams to update this information at regular intervals: perhaps yearly by routine, when a resident returns from an emergency room, hospital, or nursing home, and whenever the staff or family notices a change in behavior, health, or level of independence.

\*\*\*\*\*\*\*\*\*\*\*\*\*\*\*\*\*\*\*\*\*\*\*\*\*\*\*\*\*\*\*

In one ALF, I taught the admissions staff how to perform a simple mental-status examination. They found several applicants with memory loss and urged these families to have complete examinations before admission. Many applicants proved too confused for the facility. The staff admitted they would have accepted those applicants had they not learned how to perform the simple screening test.

\*\*\*\*\*\*\*\*\*\*\*\*\*\*\*\*\*\*\*\*\*\*\*\*\*\*\*\*\*\*\*

The cost of private-pay memory units is out of reach for many families. For publicly-funded senior housing programs or those that base fees on income, state regulations will have to change to allow these communities to:

- Designate a special wing or floor for residents who need more supervision because of memory loss.

- "Staff up" with specially trained nurses and assistants and develop appropriate activities only on those units.

- Provide ongoing training to help staff understand the conditions, manage common problems, and identify warning signs that can prevent emergencies.

- Train staff in behavior management and appropriate activities for these residents.

- Design or rearrange the environment to provide secure but unrestricted areas for residents who wander.

- Develop policies that identify a legal advocate for people who cannot make their own decisions.

Even when a facility cannot support special units, they can provide better monitoring. Advance practice professionals can come into the facility for one or two sessions per week to examine residents on a regular schedule. They can also offer urgent appointments to address new problems and teach staff how to recognize the early signs of illness. The facility does not have to pay for these services when the professionals bill Medicare or supplemental health insurance plans. Advance practice professionals can do this in collaboration with physicians or on their own in states that allow independent practice.

ALFs can use computerized pharmacy programs that monitor medicines and send alerts about routine tests, allergies, and drug interactions according to the instructions of each resident's health care team. Facilities could improve medication monitoring at no cost if they offered training opportunities for pharmacy students (with faculty supervision). This would also increase pharmacists' experience in geriatrics.

These changes would be good for everyone. Any of the recommendations would protect residents and give families and staff peace of mind. These strategies could also benefit healthier seniors who may be disturbed by neighbors whose agitation or illness is currently undiagnosed or untreated.

Adopting these suggestions can also work to maintain the census. Hospital systems are beginning to consider affiliating with facilities that offer monitoring and on-site, non-emergency care. To avoid financial penalties for unnecessary days in the hospital, these systems may stop referring patients to ALFs and nursing homes that just send residents to emergency rooms.

My conversations with staff in these communities have led me to believe that they would welcome these changes. They take pride in their work and many say they do not believe they can do their jobs well under the current limitations.

## You Are Still the Advocate

You have to advocate for your seniors when they move from the hospital to an ALF. Do not assume that emergency room physicians and hospital staff understand the difference between ALFs and nursing homes. It can be dangerous for residents to come to these facilities in the evening or on weekends if no registered nurses are on duty to carry out doctors' orders or monitor care plans. Even if the senior qualifies for skilled nursing services under Medicare, not all home health agencies can provide urgent services. Several days can pass before the first visit. If the agency can provide same-day care, *remember*, the nurses will usually visit less than an hour at a time, one to three days per week, for an average of four to six weeks. That's all.

Many pharmacy services cannot respond to changes in a medicine list in less than seventy-two hours. This can be especially dangerous if the senior needs antibiotics to treat an infection or new prescriptions to control heart failure, blood sugars, or blood pressure. If your loved one needs urgent medicines, immediate and ongoing nursing support, family members will have to fill prescriptions and stay with the senior to manage the care transition or hire private-duty nurses.

ALFs can be lifesavers when it is no longer safe for a senior to live alone and when the facility's resources *match* the residents' needs. These communities are designed for relatively healthy seniors who have few resources to help them stay in the community. ALF programs are great at providing meals, activities, socialization, transportation, and housekeeping however, they are *not* nursing homes. These facilities do not have twenty-four-hour nursing staff or medical monitoring because the law does not allow these facilities to give *care*.

Many families believe these facilities will meet all the senior's needs and allow caregivers to focus on their jobs and families without worry. Unfortunately, in most of these communities, *at night, your seniors will be as alone (without support, assistance, and supervision) as they would be in their own homes.*

The health and well-being of residents in ALFs depend on the family. Disasters can occur when a family's relief encourages them to forget that *these facilities are not nursing homes. They are neither mandated, allowed, nor equipped to provide* care. It is important to have a realistic picture of the facility's resources and decide whether those resources are right for your senior before your loved one moves in.

## So, What Do I Do?

Protect your loved ones by working with an experienced doctor or geriatrics team to understand exactly how much care your senior needs. (*See Chapter 4: Don't Despair - The Level of Care Prescription [LOCRx]*). A professional eldercare consultant can help you match the care needs and financial resources to the services and limitations of the available facilities.

If you choose to use an ALF and your senior needs more supervision or medical care than the facility can offer, you will either do it yourself, pay the facility to do it, or hire workers privately. Be sure to ask what the facility allows and add these additional costs to the price the admissions team quotes.

Do your homework. Talk to friends, families, and social workers. Visit the facilities and ask about the specific services your loved one needs. A strong relationship with a primary care physician is as important in an ALF as in any other site. Whether the doctor comes to the building or caregivers take the senior to the office, the family and the professional should have regular discussions to be sure the senior is still appropriate for the community. Since the facility staff does not usually monitor residents, families should be alert for changes in health or function and consult the doctor right away.

Unfortunately, despite the growing number of frail seniors with complex chronic conditions and extensive care needs, the number of doctors trained in geriatrics is not keeping pace.

# CHAPTER 19

# Is There a Doctor in the House? *Why Aren't There Enough Geriatricians?*

Caregivers always tell me how difficult it is to find doctors with expertise in geriatrics. This is because the aging of America has not brought an equal surge in the number of geriatrics professionals.

Despite the growing number of older adults, in 2016 there were approximately 7500 geriatricians.[45] There were more than 31,000 cardiologists (heart specialists) in a 2018 report in which geriatricians were not even listed.[46] Public policy analysts estimate that one geriatrician can care for 700 seniors. It is not clear to me how they arrived at that number however, if we accept this calculation, to meet the needs of the growing senior population, the United States must add more than 4000 geriatricians to the number we currently produce each year.[47]

I have not seen data on the number of geriatricians who are nearing retirement or have moved out of the field of aging. Based on information from the people who started when I did, that number may be significant. Several factors interact to decrease the number of geriatricians.

## An Unending Cycle Threatens the Geriatrics Workforce

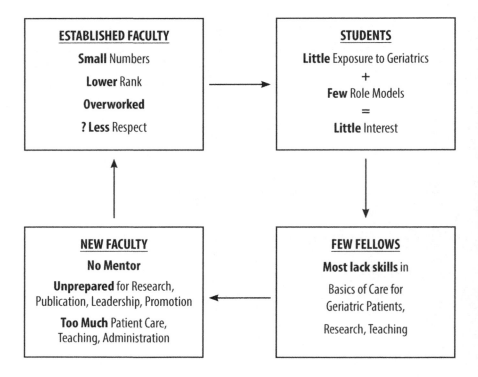

## There are Too Few Geriatricians to Teach Doctors

After four years of medical school, students choose additional training in a specialty (like Family Medicine, Internal (adult) Medicine, Surgery, or Gynecology) and complete several more years of training as interns and residents. Then, they can choose additional years as fellows in a specific subspecialty (like Cardiology, Geriatrics, or Orthopedic Surgery). Students choose specialties and subspecialties because they had classes in those subjects and developed relationships with respected mentors.

In 2017, only about forty-six percent of the geriatrics fellowship positions available in the US were filled.[48] Medical schools struggle to recruit the few geriatricians who complete fellowship training each year. With so few geriatrics professors, many students finish medical school and residency without exposure to geriatrics or geriatricians. Therefore, few doctors choose geriatrics as a career. Therefore, few doctors choose geriatrics as a career and those that do are at a disadvantage compared to fellows in other subspecialties.

## Geriatricians Start Out Behind

Physicians-in-training learn direct patient-care mostly in hospitals. They spend most of that time in intensive care units where they focus on using technology to treat sudden episodes of illness. Even their outpatient time is usually spent in hospital-based clinics. Geriatricians must also learn care for people with long-standing conditions that technology cannot cure. These patients do not necessarily benefit from being in the hospital and need to avoid unnecessary hospital visits to remain as independent as possible in the community. This means that geriatricians must learn to work in seniors' homes, in assisted-living, in nursing homes, and other long-term care sites. We must also work in teams with other professionals (nurses, therapists, social workers, and community health and faith-based networks). Community care sites and team skills are not part of basic medical training. Though there is training about the ethics of working with people who cannot make their own decision, rarely is there emphasis on specific diseases of the elderly (like dementia), how seniors walk and take care of themselves (function), and how to work with caregivers.

When we compare geriatricians and cardiologists (heart doctors) who also care for large numbers of older adults, we see that geriatricians are at a disadvantage. Cardiologists start learning about hearts in the second or third year of medical school and continue through three years of residency training in Internal or Family Medicine. Throughout their training, cardiologists learn to take care of people in the hospitals and in the office practices where they will spend most of their careers. Most geriatrics trainees do not learn about diseases of the elderly, see a nursing home, experience a home visit, or work with care team members until they begin fellowship training (after the first seven years).

In addition to expert clinical training, fellowship programs teach the skills necessary to follow the traditional path to academic success: competing for research grants, conducting research, and publishing the results in scientific journals. The best programs also teach business administration, professional speaking, and the specifics of teaching and mentoring students. The goal is to prepare fellows to become medical school faculty members. Since they start with seven-years of experience in heart disease, cardiologists can spend the two-year fellowship becoming experts and scholars in more advanced issues in heart care. They can also learn skills in research, publishing, leadership, and mentoring. Since geriatrics fellows find themselves trying to learn basic and expert clinical information at the same time. That leaves little time to solidify the skills for academic success.

## Geriatricians Try to Climb the Academic Ladder One-Handed

Without a solid educational foundation in research and leadership, most geriatrics faculty members spend most of their time in patient care, teaching, and administration. This leaves less than twenty percent of their time for the scholarly activities (successful application for research grant, publishing and presenting research results) that academic institutions value.[49,50] Because of this, most geriatricians stay in lower academic ranks with little potential for promotion. Many leave academics all together. This leaves few senior professors to mentor new geriatrics faculty and few teachers to inspire students and prepare them for geriatrics fellowship.

Many medical schools now offer a clinician/educator promotion track. Instead of research and publication, success in this track depends on teaching, mentoring, and program development. This is intended to increase the success of faculty who do not choose research careers. Though geriatrics faculty should excel in these programs, they lack specific skills in teaching and how to develop, implement, and evaluate medical education programs. This also limits their promotion potential.

## Again, the Demographics Don't Drive the Dollars.

### Can Doctors Afford to Become Geriatricians?

In 2016, the average American medical student finished training with about $190,000 in educational debt. Twenty-five percent of them owed more than $200,000.[51] This number may not include debt from undergraduate school or other graduate programs. If two medical students marry, as many did in my class, these young families start out with double the debt.

Most geriatricians begin their training in the primary care specialties, internal medicine and family medicine. Doctors in these specialties have traditionally earned much less than cardiologists and other subspecialists.[52] Although I do not believe money is the only motivation for a doctor's career choice, it is easier to pay off that kind of debt on a subspecialty salary than on a primary care income.

### Can Doctors Afford to Stay in the Service of Seniors When There is No Gerioscope?

There aren't enough geriatricians because fewer new doctors enter the field and these ranks decrease when established geriatricians cannot afford to stay in geriatrics. While the Affordable Care Act placed a higher value on prevention, wellness, and primary care, health insurance still pays more for procedures and machines. There is no gerioscope! Geriatricians do not have any specific technology that generates income. Other doctors can increase revenue by seeing large numbers of people per day. Geriatricians cannot do this because of the time it takes to care for people with several illnesses, complex medicine schedules, a high risk of drug interactions, and physical and mental disabilities. There are also caregiver and family concerns, problems with finances, transportation, other socioeconomic issues, and difficult end-of-life decisions that require more time to navigate. In the past, Medicare did not support the extra time or the expertise needed to coordinate care with all the other professionals on the team. This financial support is beginning to come in and other health insurance companies usually follow Medicare's lead. Still, the level of reimbursement does not yet match the amount of effort required to serve these high-intensity patients and their families.

The healthcare industry is exploring new funding policies that reward quality of care, rather than the number of patients a health care professional serves. Some proposals recommend "pay for performance" protocols, which imply that declining health, frequent hospital stays, and death are always signs of poor care. In truth, despite the best care, most people with chronic conditions live through an unstoppable, downward spiral with periods of relative calm between episodes of severe illness. These episodes repeat, become more frequent, and usually need hospital treatment several times before death. Most of a geriatrician's patient base consists of people with these kinds of chronic illnesses. Geriatricians can never achieve financial stability under programs where illness and death generate penalties.

*Can Geriatricians Afford to Keep Up Their Skills?*

Every ten years, geriatricians must renew board certification by investing several hundred dollars to complete about 120 hours of study. Many also conduct months of office-based research. Then, they spend another $1500 and lose income by taking a full day away from their practices to travel to a secure facility. Here, they must scan their fingerprints after every break in an eight-hour examination based more on hospital medicine than on the specifics of Geriatrics practice. Despite this, in most states, board certification does not allow geriatricians any special privileges. Medicare and other insurance plans pay a board-certified, experienced geriatrician the same amount as a doctor right out of training. The first Geriatrics certifying exam occurred in 1988. In 2012, the American Geriatrics Society published an article on the shortfall in the Geriatrics workforce.

This report showed that a large number of geriatricians who passed that first examination had not bothered to recertify.[53] I did not find a more current report however, many of my fellow geriatricians have told me they saw no reason to renew their certifications.

## Other Health Professionals Do Not Learn Eldercare, Either

With the growing numbers of seniors, you would expect all health care professionals to learn about illnesses that especially affect older people. The Accreditation Council of Graduate Medical Education (ACGME) has worked with leaders in general medical education and the American Geriatrics Society (AGS) to strengthen the geriatrics content in training programs and licensing examinations for all doctors in medicine, surgery, and behavioral health. Even so, all training programs face the same challenge to recruit experienced geriatrics professors. They also struggle to find appropriate clinical training sites and time for geriatrics in already packed courses. I doubt that additional geriatrics training would be attractive if medical students had to add more years in training and incur additional debt.

Nursing leaders decided to phase out the Gerontological Nurse Practitioner (GNP) program in 2015. Instead of GNP, program directors chose to add eldercare to the adult medicine curriculum for nurse practitioner programs and confer a credential called Adult-Gerontology-Primary Care. One administrator said the goal was to improve the care of older adults by providing geriatrics training for all nurse practitioners in adult medicine. However, I did not find that there are plans to increase the length of the current adult nurse practitioner program. Some nursing professionals believe this approach will only dilute the geriatrics experience and decrease overall expertise.[54] I wonder whether the nursing leadership would have made this decision if the number of GNP applicants had kept pace with the growing aging population.

The University of Chicago School of Social Service Administration (SSA) is one of the most prestigious social work programs on the planet. SSA has an Older Adult Program and although they had been actively recruiting, the program went several years without any full-time faculty in Gerontology (the study of aging). (Personal communication Tanya Hines, Coordinator, October 2014) Past publications have cited similar challenges in pharmacy, rehabilitation, and other healthcare professions.

All health professional training programs and schools for lawyers, financial management professionals, and first responders will also recognize the need to increase experience with older adults.

The factors that affect doctors' ability to care for older adults must change soon. Unfortunately, even with the most optimistic predictions about the timeline, the threat to quality elder care will grow as senior ranks swell. Who will advocate for changes in public policy that will improve care for your seniors? You will. Let's talk about how.

# CHAPTER 20

## A Call To Arms:
## *Legislators Need to Know What You Need*

Eldercare professionals have been crying out to reverse past Medicare cuts, ensure proper funding in the future, and shift funds from impossible cure to compassionate care. Though the Affordable Care Act and the Centers for Medicare and Medicaid Services Innovations projects are partially a result of these efforts, we have a long way to go. We need your help. Your voice and your vote will be more powerful and you, a more effective advocate if you speak the policy-makers' language.

### Arm Yourself with Information

Join a national caregiver organization and get on the mailing list. If you have computer access, follow their Facebook pages, blogs and tweets. Also participate in on-line community conversations. Like, share, and comment often. Participate in Internet caregiver support groups and other social media forums about caregiving. Join a local caregiver support group and invite eldercare experts in your community to speak at your meetings. Have your book club choose a caregiving resource and invite an expert to lead the discussion. Area Agencies on Aging, Departments on Aging, local chapters of the Alzheimer's Association and AARP, geriatrics programs in hospitals, and medical societies can provide speakers for your meetings. Many chambers of commerce have speakers' bureaus that list members who present to local organizations either free or at minimal cost.

### You Can Make the Legislators Listen

You can find your federal legislators on the Internet at www.house.gov or www.senate.gov. You will need to know your full nine-digit zip code to access both websites. If you do not know your complete zip code, find it on the postal service website www.usps.gov. Although most legislators also have their own websites, each state has a website with information about its state legislators, their committee assignments, and voting records. Your local city or village hall can also help you find your representatives.

*Find Out About Legislative Committees.*

Concentrate on committees that handle healthcare financing, aging, or caregiver legislation. Follow how your legislators vote on the issues that concern you. Leave comments on their websites, and use your vote to support people who support seniors and caregivers.

*Organize a Community Legislative Forum*

In an election year, legislators are more likely to attend or send representatives to meet with people who vote in their districts. Invite the legislators to meet with your community group. Tell them your story. Let them know how current public policy affects you. Have you had trouble finding a doctor because many have closed practices or stopped accepting Medicare? Have you lost time from work because you cannot find affordable adult day services, home services, or respite care? Has your health, job, relationships, finances, or retirement plan suffered because of caregiving responsibilities? Tell the legislators how your situation would be different if the current policies offered more support. For example, "If there had been programs to help me with A, B would not have happened, and I would not have had to do C."

Although you want to be as specific as you can, make your presentations as concise and as visual as possible. Short personal testimonies and film clips can be very effective, as are well-coordinated, hands-on experiences. One home health agency took a local congressman on home visits to describe the limitations their nurses encounter as they try to care for seniors.

*Support Organizations Working to Convince Legislators that Seniors and Caregivers Deserve Better.*

AARP, the Caregiver Action Network, National Alliance for Caregiving, the National Academies of Science Caregiving Committee, and other organizations advocate for:

- Better training for health care and social service professionals about effective caregiver evaluation, engagement, and support

- Expanded Flexible Benefits (Flex-Ben) Programs to help working caregivers pay for eldercare

- Higher salaries, stronger benefit packages, more supportive management, training, and workplace improvements to decrease turnover among long-term care workers

- Improved funding for in-home care and adult day services

- More flexible work schedules that would benefit many workers, including caregivers

- More states using public aid funds for adult day services and in-home care (not just nursing homes) when it is safe for eligible people to receive care in the community.

- Other tax credits and benefits for caregivers (Some states now allow caregivers to use their sick time and other personal time off for eldercare, but if caregivers use PTO for caregiving, what do *they* do when they are sick?)

- Research to develop the most effective ways to assess the roles, responsibilities, needs, and capabilities of caregivers

*Urge Legislators to Support More Geriatrics Training*

Many healthcare leaders hoped that if reform efforts deemphasized invasive hospital care and supported quality of life and community-based services more graduating doctors would choose careers in primary care. Many more schools include team care in the curriculum and offer clinician-educator promotion pathways. Geriatrics leaders have partnered with ACGME and medical educators to increase basic geriatrics training for all doctors and include more geriatrics on all licensing and certifying examinations. Some funding foundations also offer grants to programs that improve geriatrics education for experienced healthcare professionals. Contact your legislators to encourage their support for programs that empower professionals to enter and stay in the service of seniors. These may include:

- New healthcare financing strategies that increase payment for the type of work geriatricians do: preventative primary care and wellness services, patient education, care coordination/team care, and compassionate discussions at the end of life

- Forgiveness of educational debt for students who choose careers in aging and primary care (medicine, nursing, social work, behavioral health, pharmacy, dentistry, rehabilitation specialties), as well as healthcare administration, elder law, architecture and building design, eldercare public policy and other fields that have impact on improving the role of seniors in our society

- Grants for professional educational programs, especially those that support collaborative training in the healthcare areas listed above and in community eldercare service organizations

*Join an Organization that Advocates for Seniors and Caregivers.*

Contact your local or state Department on Aging, Area Agency on Aging, or chapter of AARP. You can find other healthcare policy activist groups through the community outreach departments of most hospitals. Volunteer with the local, state, or federal agencies that focus on an aspect of caregiving that affects or interests you (for example, working caregivers, grandparents raising children, finances, elder abuse and neglect, or the ombudsman program). Become active in associations that advocate for people with illnesses that affects your family. Area agencies on aging, the Alzheimer's Association, and other illness-specific organizations may have community advisory boards that would benefit from your energy and expertise.

There is so much work to do in this area. Congress is considering more extensive programs to aid family caregivers and legislators need to hear your voice to make changes that will really help.

## Get Involved! You CAN Make a Difference!

# CONCLUSION

**Effective caregivers** seek information about care options, organize personal health information, and work with a team of professionals and other helpers to give excellent care. These caregivers learn the specific questions to ask at each care site, and they understand the power of always speaking and behaving in a professional manner.

**Fearless caregivers** get professional help when feelings of guilt, anger, uncertainty, disappointment, unforgiveness, or depression interfere with good caregiving.

**Healthy caregivers** understand the difference between *selfish* and *self-care*. They believe they deserve to have joy, healthy relationships, time for themselves, physical, financial, emotional, and spiritual health.

**Law-abiding caregivers** understand that using seniors' money for *anything* other than their direct care is committing the crime of elder abuse in the category of financial exploitation.

**Sensible caregivers** manage their finances and plan to make their own twilight years truly golden. They also arrange their affairs so that caregiving responsibilities will not crush their adult children.

**Smart caregivers** encourage all adult family members to discuss their wishes and prepare advance directives to document the quality of life they would want in a life-changing illness.

**Strong caregivers** work with other eldercare experts to raise awareness of caregiving needs and encourage legislators to enact more helpful public policy.

*Please* stop feeling guilty because you think you're not as good a caregiver as your mother was. She dealt with apples; you're dealing with oranges. She did not have to take care of so many seniors; those seniors didn't live so long and they didn't have the chronic conditions and disabilities you're fighting. She probably had more siblings, lived closer to her elders, and did not have to juggle as many other responsibilities as you do.

It's easy to feel overwhelmed, yet there are ways to feel (and to *be*) in control. Find a geriatrics program to prescribe the LOCRx, so you are clear about what your senior needs. Work with eldercare consultants and social service experts to develop and monitor a care plan that meets those needs. The strongest plan will also respect the values of your senior and your family in developing goals and investigating resources. Commit to staying in charge of the care plan as an informed, effective partner with your seniors and your professional advisers.

Remember the Five Keys to Caregiver Survival:

1) Don't Put Your Head in the Sand. *Find out if you need help.*

2) Take the "S" Off Your Chest or Step Away from the Kryptonite. *You DO need help.*

3) Don't Ask; Don't Tell Won't Work. *Tell people you need help.*

4) If You Don't Want to Drive All the Time, Take Your Hands off the Steering Wheel. *Let people help.*

5) Put YOUR Mask on FIRST. *You Can't Take Care of Them if You Don't Take Care of YOU* (This final Key recalls what flight attendants tell you to do in an emergency).


You are your senior's primary and most precious resource. Commit to taking care of yourself.


### Don't Say You Don't Have Time.

You have every moment God has given you; you need to be a good steward of those moments. You deserve joy and health. You must take time to learn what you need to know, identify your team members, and get the help you need to take care of your seniors without destroying yourself. Many of the caregiver stories I've shared in this book show caregivers with damaged health, eroded joy, or lives cut short. If you don't make time for yourself now, like those who did not survive caregiving, you can step into eternity sooner than you wish. What a waste of wonderful YOU!

You deserve to take care of you for YOU but if I haven't convinced you of that, do it for your seniors. If you die (or become disabled), what will happen to your senior?

Since you've walked with me through these pages, you know which tools will empower you to give excellent eldercare without injuring yourself. Pick up your tools and keep creating joy as you advocate for your senior, yourself, and tomorrow's caregivers. Get the job done but remember: *The best gift you can give your loved one is a healthy, balanced, knowledgeable caregiver.*

You cannot give care, supervise care, or advocate for anyone when you are afraid and uninformed, physically ill, financially strapped, emotionally exhausted, or spiritually bankrupt.

Taking care of you *is* taking care of them.


**You CAN do this! I'm here to help you.**
Visit my website, www.drcherylwoodson.com, to share your questions and comments. Since I cannot respond to every message, I'll settle for addressing as many questions as I can in my blog, "Straight Talk with Dr. Cheryl. Also, please Like my Dr. *Cheryl Woodson Facebook* page, my videos, and podcasts on YouTube and Instagram. I'll update you about new publications and events where we can meet in person as soon as it's safe.

Be sure to find a caregiver support group online or in your community. We're stronger when we share our wisdom and take care of each other.

*We CAN do this together!*

# REFERENCES

1.  Administration on Community Living and Administration on Aging of the US Department of Health and Human Services, *2019 Profile of Older Americans*, 22, July 2020 acl.gov/aging-and-disability-in-america/data-and-research/profile-older-americans (accessed 27 July 2020)

2.  Heimlich, Russell, Baby Boomers Retire, www.pewresearch.org/fact-tank/2010/12/29/baby-boomers-retire/ (accessed 7 June 2018)

3.  Life Expectancy in the US 1900-1998 www.u.demog.berkeley.edu/~andrew/1918/figure2.html (accessed 7 June 2018)

4.  US Department of Health and Human Services, Centers for Disease Control and Prevention, National Centers for Health Statistics, *Health United States 2016*, DHHS Publication 2017-1231, May 2017, Life expectancy at birth, at age 65, and at age 75, by sex, race, and Hispanic origin: United States, selected years 1900–2015, Table 15 (page 1 of 2). pg 131. www.cdc.gov/nchs/data/hus/hus16.pdf#015 (accessed 7 June 2018)

5.  Xu, J, Mortality Among Centenarians 2000-2014, National Center for Health Statistics Brief Number 223, January 2016 (updated June 28, 2016) www.cdc.gov/nchs/data/databriefs/db233.pdf (accessed 7 June 2018)

6.  Centers for Disease Control and Prevention, National Centers for Health Statistics, Leading Causes of Death 2016, FastFacts

Homepage, March 2017 www.cdc.gov/nchs/fastats/leading-causes-of-death.htm (accessed 7 June 2018)

7. Centers for Disease Control and Prevention, National Centers for Health Statistics, Leading Causes of Death 1900-1998 Pg 67 www.cdc.gov/nchs/data/dvs/lead1900_98.pdf (accessed 7 June 2018)

8. Administration on Community Living and Administration on Aging of the US Department of Health and Human Services, *2019 Profile of Older Americans*, 22, July 2020 www.acl.gov/aging-and-disability-in-america/data-and-research/profile-older-americans (accessed 27 July 2020)

9. Hochschild, A, Machungh, A, *The Second Shift: Working Families ad the Revolution at Home*, Penguin Books (revised edition), January 31, 2012

10. AARP and National Alliance for Caregiving. Caregiving in the United States 2020. Washington, DC: AARP. May 2020. www.doi.org/10.26419/ppi.00103.003 , (accessed 10 June 2020)

11. Schulz, R, and Eden, J Editors; Committee on Family Caregiving for Older Adults; Board on Health Care Services; Health and Medicine Division; National Academies of Sciences, Engineering, and Medicine. 2016 *Families Caring for an Aging America,* pg 49, Washington, DC: The National Academies Press. doi: 10.17226/23606

12. Ellis, RR and Simmons, T, Co-resident Grandparents and their Grandchildren, Population Characteristics www.census.gov/content/dam/Census/library/publications/2014/demo/p20-576.pdf (accessed 9 June 2018)

13. Woolley, S, Rise of Gray Divorce Forces Financial Reckoning After 50, www.bloomberg.com/news/articles/2018-04-13/rise-of-gray-divorce-forces-financial-reckoning-after-50 (accessed 7 June 2018)

14. Aging Parents: 8 Warning Signs of Health Problems." www.mayoclinic.org/healthy-lifestyle/caregivers/in-depth/aging-parents/art-20044126 13 December 2017 (accessed 8 August 2018)

15. AARP Bulletin, 1 May 2012 "The Most Common Reasons for Hospital Admissions for in Older Adults. <www.aarp.org/doctors-hospitals/info> Retrieved 8 August 2013

16. "Ask Me 3," National Patient Safety Foundation (www.npsf.org)

17. Evans, J, *Marriage on the Rock*, Improv, Ltd. 2011

18. Exodus 20:12, *The Holy Bible, King James Version*

19. Ephesians 6:1, *The Holy Bible, King James Version*

20. James 4:2, *The Holy Bible, King James Version*

21. Schulz, R, and Eden, J, Editors; Committee on Family Caregiving for Older Adults; Board on Health Care Services; Health and Medicine Division; National Academies of Sciences, Engineering, and Medicine. 2016 *Families Caring for an Aging America,* Fig.3-4, pg 94, Washington, DC: The National Academies Press. doi: 10.17226/23606

22. AARP and National Alliance for Caregiving. Caregiving in the United States 2020. Washington, DC: AARP. May 2020. www.doi.org/10.26419/ppi.00103.003 , (accessed 10 June 2020)

23. Jones, L.B. *Jesus in Blue Jeans, A Practical Guide to Everyday Spirituality,* pp.28-31, New York, NY: Hyperion, 2011.

24. ibid. pp.12-15

25. Truman, Karol K. *Feelings Buried Alive Never Die.* 1991 Phoenix, AZ: Olympus Distributing, 2003.

26. Cade, Eleanor. *Taking Care of Parents Who Didn't Take Care of You: Making Peace with Aging Parents.* Century City, MN: Hazelden Publishing and Educational Services, 2000.

27. Miller, A. *The Drama of the Gifted Child: The Search for the True Self.* New York, NY: Basic Books, 1997., anniversary edition 2008

28. Jeffress, R. *When Forgiveness Doesn't Make Sense.* Colorado Springs, CO: Water Brook Press, 2008.

29. Evans, J. *Marriage on the Rock, God's Design for Your Dream Marriage.* "Skills for In-Law Relations, Number One: The Principle of Honor," pp267-69. Zondervan Corporation, Grand Rapids, MI, 2005.

30. Gibran, K. "On Children," *The Prophet.* 1923. New York, NY: Alfred Knopf, Inc., 2001. 17-18.

31. Jakes, T.D. "Never Give Up." audiotape ministry. <www.tdjakes.org>.

32. Siegel, Bernie. *Love, Medicine & Miracles, Lessons Learned About Self-Healing from A Surgeon*

33. Meyer C: "Allow Natural Death An Alternative to DNR?" Hospice Patients Alliance Website. 2014.www.hospicepatients.org/and.

html (Last accessed December 10, 2018)

34. National POLST Paradigm www.polst.org/, Retrieved 13 August 2018

35. Amount of Time Primary Care Physicians Spend with Each Patient, Statistica- The Statistics Portal www.statista.com/statistics/250219/us-physicians-opinion-about-their-compensation/ (accessed 11 Aug 2018)

36. The Adult Day Services Program (with PMD Advisory Services, LLC & Seniors Research Group of Market Strategies, Inc.) "A National Study of Adult Day Services by Partners in Caregiving," 2002. www.rwjf.org/newsroom/featureDetail.jwp?featureID=1838pageNum=48type=3 (initially accessed 26 July 2006)

37. *MetLife National Study of Adult Day Services: Providing Support to Individuals and their Family Caregivers*, National Adult Day Services Association (NASDA), Ohio State University, College of Social Work, MetLife Mature Market Institute, 2010

38. Bureau of Labor Statistics. "Occupational outlook Handbook," www.bls.gov/ooh/healthcare/nursing-assistants.htm 18 April 2018 and www.bls.gov/ooh/food-preparation-and-serving/food-and-beverage-serving-and-related-workers.htm 13 April 2018 (both accessed 8 August 2018).

39. Matthew, M, Carsten, MK, Ayers, DJ, Menahem, N, Determinants of turnover among low-wage earners in long term care: the role of manager-employer relationships, *Geriatric Nursing*, 39:4, 2018, pp 407-413

40. Reinhard, S, Feinberg, LF, Choula, R, Houser, A, "Valuing the Invaluable 2015: Undeniable Progress but Big Gaps Remain," AARP Public Policy Update, www.aarp.org/ppi/info-2015/valuing-the-invaluable-2015-update.html?cmp=RDRCT-VALUN_JUN23_015?intcmp=AE-BL-IL-DOTORG July 16, 2015 (accessed 4 August 2018).

41. Schulz, R, and Eden, J, Editors; Committee on Family Caregiving for Older Adults; Board on Health Care Services; Health and Medicine Division; National Academies of Sciences, Engineering, and Medicine. 2016 *Families Caring for an Aging America*, pg 127 Washington, DC: The National Academies Press. doi: 10.17226/23606

42. Eisenberg, R, "The Financial and Personal Toll of Family Caregiving," Forbes, March 12, 2018, www.forbes.com/sites/nextavenue/2018/03/12/the-financial-and-personal-toll-of-family-caregiving/#615111e358b8 (accessed 4 August 2018)

43. Bengal, G., "Doctors Refuse to Accept Medicare Patients, Health IT Outcomes," www.healthitoutcomes.com/doc/doctors-refuse-to-accept-medicare-patients-0001 August 9, 2013, Accessed 7 17 2018

44. Olivero, M, "Doctor Shortage. Who Will Take Care of the Elderly?" US News and World Report- Health, April 21, 2015, www.health.usnews.com/health-news/patient-advice/articles/2015/04/21/doctor-shortage-who-will-take-care-of-the-elderly, (accessed 13 August 2018

45. "Number of Active Physicians in the US 2018 by Specialty Area," Statistica-the Statistics Portal www.statista.com/statistics/209424/us-number-of-active-physicians-by-specialty-area/ (accessed 13 August 2018)

46. Olivero, M, "Doctor Shortage. Who Will Take Care of the Elderly?" US News and World Report- Health, April 21, 2015, www.health.usnews.com/health-news/patient-advice/articles/2015/04/21/doctor-shortage-who-will-take-care-of-the-elderly, (accessed 13 August 2018

47. "Results and Data Specialties Matching Service®2018 Appointment Year" February 2018The MATCH National Resident Matching Program www.nrmp.org accessed 13 August 2018

48. "Ratio of Physician Faculty FTE (full-time equivalents) in Geriatrics to Students Indicates Need for Title VII Programs, GWPS, Detailed Data on Geriatrics Workforce," 2012, AGS < www.amerianGeriatrics.org>, Retrieved 9 September 2013

49. "Allocation of Faculty and Staff Time 2001, 2005, 2007, 2008, 2010, Table 2.1, Survey of Academic Leaders in Geriatrics at US Medical Schools," GWPS Detailed Data on Geriatrics Workforce, 2012, AGS <www.americanGeriatrics.org > Retrieved 9 September 2012

50. "Average Medical School Debt in 2017" Student Debt Relief July 26, 2018, www.studentdebtrelief.us/news/average-medical-school-debt/ (accessed 13 August 2018)

51. "Medscape Physician Compensation Report 2018," www.medscape.com/slideshow/2018-compensation-overview-6009667 (accessed 1 August 2018

52. The American Geriatrics Society, "Current Geriatrician Shortfall," <www.americanGeriatrics.org/files/documents/Adv_Resources/ GeriShortfallCurrentNumbers/2012.pdf >, retrieved 9 September 2013 (re-accessed 13 February 2018)

53. Villars, Patrice, "Death of Gerontological Nurse Practitioner, Pt 1," in *GEriPal A Geriatrics & Palliative Care Blog* www.geripal. org/2012/05/death-of-gerontological nurse.html, retrieved 5 March 2014. (re-accessed 13 February 2018)

# RESOURCES

**Download these free materials from www.drcherylwoodson.com**

You Should Know These Numbers Like You Know Your Social Security Number (questions to review with your doctor every year)

Instructions for Creating Bernie Ryan's Binder

Dr. Woodson's Medication Sheet

## BOOKS

Adams, J, *When Our Grown Kids Disappoint Us: Letting Go of Their Problems, Loving Them Anyway, and Getting On With Our Lives*, Free Press, 2004

Beattie, Melody, *Codependent No More: How to Stop Controlling Others and Start Caring for Yourself, Hazledon Foundation*, 1989, 1992, 2001.

Beattie, Melody, *The Language of Letting Go: Daily Meditations for Codependents, 1ˢᵗ edition, Hazledon Publishing. July 1990*

Cade, Eleanor, *Taking Care of Parents Who Didn't Take Care of You: Making Peace With Aging Parents.* Century City, MN: Hazeldon Publishing and Educational Services, 2009

Codependents Anonymous, *The CoDa Book*, www.coda.org

Evans, Jimmy. *Marriage on the Rock*, Improv, Ltd. 2011

Gibran, Kahlil, *The Prophet*. 1923 New York, NY: Alfred Knopf, Inc., 2001

Greeson, Hochschild, A, Machungh, A, *The Second Shift: Working Families and the Revolution at Home*, Penguin Books (revised edition), January 31, 2012

Jeffress, Robert *When Forgiveness Doesn't Make Sense*, Colorado Springs, CO: Water Brook Press, 2013

Jones, Laurie Beth, *Jesus in Blue Jeans, A Practical Guide to Everyday Spirituality*. Hachette, 1998.

Katie, Byron and Mitchell, Stephen, *Loving What Is: Four Questions That Can Change your Life*, Harmony, 2002

Mace, NL, and Rabins, PV, *The 36-Hour Day A Family Guide to Caring for People Who Have Alzheimer's Disease, Related Dementias, and Memory Loss*, 5th ed., Grand Central & Style, 2012

Meyer, Joyce, *Approval Addiction: Overcoming Your Need to Please Everyone*, FaithWords, Nashville, TN 2005

Miller, Alice. *The Drama of the Gifted Child: The Search for the True Self*. New York, NY: Basic Books, 2008

Siegel, Bernie. *Love, Medicine & Miracles, Lessons Learned About Self-Healing From A Surgeon's Experience with Exceptional Patients*, William Morrow Paperbacks, 1998

Truman, Karol K. *Feelings Buried Alive Never Die*, Olympus Publishing, 1991.

## ORGANIZATIONS

This alphabetical list, current as of November 2018, is for your information. I do not intend it to be exhaustive and it does not constitute an endorsement of any service or program. Please do your homework before you contract for any services.

### Caregiving and Eldercare Information and Support Services

AARP www.aarp.org (888) OUR AARP, (888) 687-2277

AARP Caregiving Resources www.aarp.org/home-family/caregiving/prepare-to-care-planning-guide.html

Smart Driver™ Program (register for online course and find a class in your area) www.aarp.org/auto/driver-safety/

Aging Life Care Association, Inc. (formerly the National Association of Professional Geriatric Care Managers) www.aginglifecare.org, (520) 881-8008

American Geriatrics Association (AGS) www.americanGeriatrics.org, (212) 308-1414

American Medical Association (AMA) www.ama-assn.org, (800) 621-8335

American Medical Association: Physician's Guide to Assessing and Counseling Older Drivers 2005

A Place for Mom, www.aplaceformom.com, (800) 621-8335

Caregiver Action Network, (Formerly National Association of Family Caregivers), www.caregiveraction.org, (202) 454-3970

Codependents Anonymous (www.coda.org)

Eldercare Locator-Administration on Aging (AoA), www.eldercare.acl.gov/Public/Index.aspx (800) 677-1116

Family Caregiver Alliance, www.caregiver.org, (800) 445-8106

Leeza's Care Connection (formerly The Leeza Gibbons Memory Foundation), www.leezascareconnectionorg, (888) OK LEEZA, 1(888) 655-3392, infor@leezascareconnection.org

Mrs. Dorothy Peterson: A Case Study: Lutheran General Health System, to purchase a copy of the video, visit and search www.terranova.org or www.worldcat.org

National Adult Protective Services Association (NAPSA) and the National APS Resource Center, www.napsa-now.org, (202) 370-6292

National Alliance for Caregiving, www.caregiving.org

National Association of Area Agencies on Aging, www.n4a.org,     (202) 872-0888

National Association of Elder law Attorneys (NAELA), www.naela.org

National Association of Personal Financial Advisors (NAPFA) www.napfa.org (888) FEE-ONLY (888-333-6659)

National Center on Elder Abuse, Administration on Aging www.ncea.acl.gov, (855) 500 3537 (ELDR)

National Center for the Prevention of Elder Abuse www.preventelderabuse.org (site update in progress)

National Council on Aging (NCOA) www.ncoa.org, (571) 527-3900

National Foundation for Credit Counseling (NFCC) www.nfcc.org (800) 388 2227, En Español (844) 359-3825

Institute for HealthCare Improvement National Patient Safety Foundation "Ask Me 3," www.ihi.org/resources/Pages/Tools/Ask-Me-3-Good-Questions-for-Your-Good-Health.aspx

Today's Caregiver Magazine, www.caregiver.com

**Organizations for Specific Health Conditions**

These groups provide information, promote health, support research and education about these common illnesses, and often have specific information for caregivers. There are many other condition-specific organizations. The Internet will guide you to the ones that focus on conditions that challenge you and your family.

Alzheimer's Association, www.alz.org, (800) 272-3900 (24hr hotline)

American Cancer Society, www.cancer.org, (800) ACS-2345, (800) 227-2345

American Diabetes Association, www.diabetes.org, (800) DIABETES, (800) 342-2383

American Heart Association, www.heart.org, (800) AHA-USA1, (800) 242-8721

American Lung Association, www.lung.org, (800) LUNGUSA (800) 586-4872

American Stroke Association, www.strokeassociation.org, (888) 4 STROKE, (888) 478-7653 En Español (888) 474-VIVE

Arthritis Foundation, www.arthritis.org, Helpline (844) 571-4357

National Kidney Foundation, www.kidney.org, 1(855) NKF-CARES, (855) 653-2273 or (800) 622-9010

National Multiple Sclerosis Society,www.nationalmssociety.org, (800) FIGHT MS, (800) 344-4867

National Osteoporosis Foundation, www.nof.org, (800) 231-4222

National Parkinson Foundation, www.parkinson.org, (800) 4PD-INFO

National Stroke Association, www.stroke.org, (800) STROKES, (800) 787-6537

# Acknowledgments

Like the first edition of *TO SURVIVE CAREGIVING*, this book is dedicated to my Father, my family, friends, and colleagues. I am so grateful for their love, patience, and support.

Special thanks go to people without whom the second edition might never have happened:

- Kathryn Kraynick challenged me to articulate the book's true purpose and showed me how to let it go.

- Adrienne D. Mims, MD, MPH advised me with love and masterful bullying.

- Jeannette E. South-Paul, MD Col., MC (RET) (aka Bess,) gave hard truths with hugs and warm fuzzies.

- Joy Shields from The Writer's Beacon, Liz Ridley from The Writer's Midwife, and Brittiany Koren of Written Dreams, tightened the editing over the years.

- Mirella Tovar of MeToo Designs, Blue Island, IL, designed the front cover and L. Julie Torrey Parker did additional back-cover design.

- My sister-in-law, Brackette F. Williams, PhD, took time out from being a genius to do the copy editing.

- My friend and former boss, Doris Mitchell Green, my partner, Robert F. Watt, and my daughter, Lauren C.H. Murff, did the proofreading.

Also, as I did in the first edition, I dedicate this book to the caregivers I have known in over thirty years of medical practice. Thank you for teaching me and trusting me with your health, your loved ones, and your stories.

# About the Author

Dr. Woodson has spent more than thirty years teaching and practicing Geriatric Medicine while raising a family. For ten of those years, she also navigated her mother's journey with Alzheimer's disease. Dr. Cheryl brings a unique perspective: a professional's expertise, tempered by a daughter's practical understanding, offered in the plain speaking of a Sagittarian from North Philadelphia.

An informative, inspiring, and entertaining speaker whom the *New York Times* called "a blunt and funny woman," Dr. Cheryl shoots from the hip and from the heart to support family caregivers and the professionals who counsel them to give excellent eldercare without damaging their health, finances, and relationships.

For more information, to hear about new publications and events, or to schedule a presentation or interview, visit www.drcherylwoodson. com. You can also follow her blog, Straight Talk with Dr. Cheryl, visit her YouTube Channel, and follow her on Facebook, Instagram, and TikTok.

Be sure to look for the companion book *The Doctor is IN: Answering Your Questions about How to Survive Caregiving*, for more in-depth information about specific questions caregivers have asked Dr. Cheryl. It is available, now, at your favorite book seller.

Made in United States
North Haven, CT
23 August 2023

40651778R00134